I0890220

Speculative Fictions

ILLUMINATIONS: CULTURAL FORMATIONS OF THE AMERICAS

John Beverley and Sara Castro-Klarén, Editors

SPECULATIVE FICTIONS

Chilean Culture, Economics, and the Neoliberal Transition

ALESSANDRO FORNAZZARI

UNIVERSITY OF PITTSBURGH PRESS

Published by the University of Pittsburgh Press, Pittsburgh, Pa., 15260

Manufactured in the United States of America

Printed on acid-free paper

10 9 8 7 6 5 4 3 2 1

Library of Congress Cataloging-in-Publication Data

Fornazzari, Alessandro, 1970–
Speculative fictions : Chilean culture, economics, and the neoliberal transition / Alessandro Fornazzari.
pages cm. – (Illuminations: cultural formations of the Americas)
ISBN 978-0-8229-6233-5 (pbk.)
1. Neoliberalism—Chile. 2. Culture—Economic aspects—Chile. 3. Chile—Civilization—20th century. 4. Chilean literature—20th century—History and criticism. 5. Chile—Intellectual life—20th century. 6. National characteristics, Chilean. I. Title.
HC192.F67 2013
330.983—dc23 2013003758

CONTENTS

Acknowledgments *vii*

Introduction 1

1. The Brooder's Startled Gaze: José Donoso, Broken Allegories, and the Commodity Form 13
2. Literature and Labor: Post-Fordism and Human Capital in Diamela Eltit and Arturo Fontaine 39
3. Restitution, Memory, and the Market: The Chilean Documentary 63
4. Critical Visuality or Global Subsumption? Neoliberal Biopolitics, Chilean Visual Arts, and the Economic Text 87
5. Reflections on a Residual Formation: Intellectual Work, Real Subsumption, and Socialized Labor 106

Notes *119*

Bibliography *139*

Index *151*

ACKNOWLEDGMENTS

The ground for this project was prepared at least as far back as 1995 at a conference in Santiago that Alberto Moreiras participated in while I was a student at the Universidad de Chile. The talk Alberto gave is now a widely cited and influential piece of the postdictatorship archive, and it proved to be particularly influential for me because it motivated me to go to North Carolina to study with him. I thank him for his mentorship and for being a model of intellectual generosity.

The book itself materialized in a context that I remember fondly as being charged with intense debates, workshops, collaborations, frenzied readings, and late-night conversations. The following people helped me think through the problems I explore in this book: Idelber Avelar, Jon Beasley-Murray, John Beverley, Oscar Cabezas, Elizabeth Collingwood-Selby, Ariel Dorfman, Patrick Dove, Federico Galende, Kate Jenckes, Adriana Johnson, John Kraniauskas, Marta Hernández-Salván, Horacio Legrás, Ryan Long, Gabriela Nouzeilles, Juan Poblete, Juan Carlos Rodríguez, Freya Schiwy, Willy Thayer, Teresa Vilarós, Gareth Williams, and Sergio Villalobos-Ruminott.

Two other groups made key intellectual contributions to this project. I am grateful to the members of the John Hope Franklin Seminar "Race, Justice, and the Politics of Memory" (Srinivas Aravamudan, Ian Baucom, J. Kameron Carter, Sheila Dillon, Grant Farred, Thavolia Glymph, Evelyn Brooks Higginbotham, Charles Piot, Leigh Raiford, Stephane Robolin, and Susan Thorne), who, among other things, helped me see that I had become too comfortable in my area studies perspective. My colleagues at the University of California Riverside, Susan Antebi, Jodi Kim, Miriam Lam, Vorris Nunley, and Freya Schiwy, provided much-needed feedback at a crucial moment in the book's development.

I will always be grateful to Freya and Cassandra, who not only endured my moods while I was writing this book but made life wonderful. This book is dedicated to my parents and my grandmother Victoria Batista Reed.

Speculative Fictions

INTRODUCTION

When the Chilean philosopher Patricio Marchant reflects on why after fifteen years of university life dedicated to studying philosophy and psychoanalysis, he decided to devote himself to Gabriela Mistral's poetry (producing the singular encounter between theoretical thinking and Mistral that is the book *Sobre arboles y madres*), he recalls a gift given to him many years earlier by his first philosophy teacher: "your duty," Louis-Bertrand Geiger advised him, "is to study what is great in your *patria,* Chilean poetry."[1] For Marchant this duty—a joyful one, a celebration—is distinct from the kind of intellectual work emanating from the will to knowledge that motivates university discourse. It is, rather, the acceptance of a duty assigned to him as a subject from a place, a language, and a history. No doubt that today Chilean poetry continues to be a rich and joyful duty that calls for our study; but from the perspective of our current historical conjuncture—the crisis of neoliberalism—one of the strong contributions that the Chilean experience of the last forty years has to make to contemporary critical-theoretical discourse in the humanities is a unique insight into the culture, problems, and logics of the transition to neoliberal capitalism. The duty of this study then is to give an account of this transitional experience.[2]

Frequently heralded as the first project of neoliberal state formation and one of the great modern laboratories of political and economic experimentation, the Chilean dictatorship and postdictatorship period is, almost by antonomasia, linked to terms such as *structural adjustment, economic shock treatment,* and the *economic miracle* and to a series of economic reforms that have become hypostatized under the general rubric of neoliberalism. This transitional moment—understood in Willy Thayer's sense as the passage from the sovereignty of the state to the sovereignty of the market—marks a moment of capital flight. Capital disengages from the factories and industries (the spaces of extraction and production associated with an earlier regime of capital accumulation, import-substitution industrialization) and concentrates on speculative sites such as investments, mortgages, currency contracts, corporate securities, and the stock market.[3] Tomás Moulian identifies accelerated deindustrialization and the massification of credit as the defining characteristics of the Chilean transitional period. He goes on to claim that they led to a new regime of "plastic money" and a new subject: "the credit card citizen."[4] How can we think the relation between culture and economics in this transitional period? Or, how do we map the effects of this financialization and the reorganization of society around consumption and communication in the realm of cultural production? The paradox that resides at the core of this question has to do with the present's inability to distinguish between these two spheres. This indistinguishability is one of the defining characteristics of neoliberalism: that is to say, the expansion of the economic form to the point that it covers the totality of the social sphere, hence eliding any difference between economics and culture.

This is the task that *Speculative Fictions* undertakes: to analyze the reconfiguration of the aesthetic and the economic spheres in the context of the Chilean neoliberal transition (1973 to the present). This book begins this task by attempting to address a problem made visible through a reading of José Donoso's *Casa de campo,* a novel that allegorizes the military coup and the neoliberal transition. I argue that in an attempt to define what kind of writing is possible after 1973, the novel reveals a double bind: it reflects on its own failure to produce a defetishizing realist discourse capable of returning us to the materiality of things, and it also reveals the failure of allegory as a form that can continue to function in a Benjaminian sense as a transitional discourse, that is, one that can gesture toward the coming of a new emergent formation. This failure of allegory to continue to function as a transitional mode of thinking is due to its logic of abstraction being exceeded and rendered obsolete by the commodity form.[5] My reading of José Donoso's novel suggests that the allegorical fragment having been rendered obsolete by capital's globalizing logic can no longer account for the cultural forms related to neoliberal capitalism. Working with novels, essays, documentaries, *testimonios,* and the visual arts, this study explores a series of emergent figures in contemporary Chilean cultural production that take up the challenge left to us by Donoso's work. These figures include: the stock-market model of value, the artist-entrepreneur, human capital and the virtuoso model of labor, commodified memory, and the *imbunche* as an economic text.

The stock-market model of value emerged as a figure during the financial boom and bust of the early 1980s. Arturo Fontaine's novel *Oír su voz,* for example, depicts the rise of a new breed of entrepreneur whose neoliberal model of value is based on the concept of human capital (the investment made in skills acquired through activities such as education, training, and hobbies in order to maximize one's value in the workplace). In this way the calculating rationality associated with previous cycles of capitalist accumulation is replaced with attributes such as high-stakes risk taking, undecidability, a valorization of creation, and virtuosity. In the age of financialization the work of the new entrepreneurs is modeled on the characteristics of creative artistic ability; they are presented as artist-entrepreneurs. From a very different perspective, Diamela Eltit's *Mano de obra* critiques post-Fordist conceptualizations of the service sector (the virtuoso model of labor).

In the context of the Chilean documentary form, commodified memory refers to the plight of memory politics during the neoliberal transition. Effectively deployed during the antidictatorship struggles, memory politics as a contestatory practice and as a resource for collective action, I argue, needs to be rethought in the age of the mass-media saturation and the "informationalization" of memory. The figure of restitution is put forward as a way of thinking about the past that moves us beyond melancholic angst and the discourse of apology, forgiveness, and repentance, in order to move toward a fuller understanding of the profound transformations produced by the coup and the transition.

The *imbunche*—a figure from Mapuche mythology that has all of its bodily orifices sewn closed by witches— which was perhaps most famously resignified in José Donoso's *El obsceno pájaro de la noche,* was taken up by the visual artist Catalina Parra in 1977 to signal how the dictatorship was producing sutured, mutilated, and censored bodies. This figure was resignified again in the neoliberal moment as a vehicle for thinking the problems of a critical visual arts practice in a time when its antiinstitutional strategies seemed to have been effectively subsumed by the speculative logic of neoliberal capitalism.

As a precursor to the adoption of the neoliberal model in other parts of the globe, the focus on Chile allows for a careful, situated, and historicized exploration of the cultural logics of neoliberal capitalism. The rationale for the emphasis on a national context is twofold: to contribute to the field of Chilean literary and cultural studies and, more ambitiously, to show what the Chilean neoliberal experience reveals about the inner logic and profound effects of the global neoliberal condition at the moment of its supposed disappearance.[6] The question then is, what can the Chilean neoliberal experience offer the world regarding our understanding of the transformations that have occurred and the kinds of antagonistic logics that are now possible?

Contextualizing Chilean Neoliberalism

The Chilean neoliberal project emerges out of a specific historical conjuncture. It becomes the dominant economic model in the aftermath of the 1973 military coup and, as such, can be seen as a reaction to the leftist policies of the Unidad Popular (Popular Unity) government.[7] But for a deeper understanding of this social and economic phenomenon, its roots need to be traced further back. A longer perspective reveals the neoliberal project to be a reaction against the system of import-substitution industrialization and the Keynesian state form that prevailed in Chile and much of Latin America since the 1930s. Out of the 1929 stock-market crash and the Great Depression this Keynesian state form emerged in Latin America, shedding many of the precrisis liberal laissez-faire principles and advocating a mixed economy with an active public sector. In Chile this transitional period of liberal trade crisis and the subsequent passage to import-substitution industrialization was marked by the end of the Ibañez regime, the collapse of the nitrates market, and the global economic recession.[8] In the context of this periodization, the 1970 Popular Unity government represents a radical incarnation of this national popular state project, while the 1973 military coup marks the end of the cycle and the violent transition to the neoliberal period.

A characteristic specific to the Chilean neoliberal transition is that the implementation of structural reforms (specifically the economic "shock" plan of 1975) preceded the adoption of this economic ideology by the International Monetary Fund and the World Bank as their official policy toward Latin America. It was only after 1983 that these institutions became actively involved in Chile.[9] This means that narratives that situate the Chilean neoliberal transition within the general context of the crisis of the national-populist Keynesian state—catalyzed in most Latin American countries by the 1982 debt crisis—end up erasing the historical specificity of the Chilean capitalist revolution. In Chile by 1982 the state-centered model had already been effectively dismantled.[10] Thus for the Chilean case, neoliberalism—understood here in its limited sense as a set of economic reforms that put into practice the Chicago School's reworking of classical economic doctrine (privatization, flexibilization of labor, "downsizing" and rationalization, deregulation and diminished capital market restrictions)—needs to be situated in relation to a longer period of economic and political transformation.[11]

The Chilean neoliberal transition is commonly periodized into two distinct stages.[12] The first—and most ideologically radical phase—began in 1975 and collapsed with the economic crisis of 1982.[13] This first stage was marked by the appointment of Chicago School–trained economists to many of the key state economic posts (Sergio de Castro's appointment as the minister of the economy was this stage's apex).[14] It was during this period that Milton Friedman's ideas were most faithfully put into practice by his Chilean students and followers. These policies included: liberalizing the price system and market, opening the country up to foreign trade, and generally reducing government involvement in the economy.[15] The second phase inaugurated a more pragmatic form of neoliberalism. This phase emerged after the economic debt crisis of the early 1980s, which sank the short-lived "Chilean economic miracle" and threatened the future of the Chilean neoliberal economic model. The resulting government bailout of private banks was lampooned by the regime's critics as the "Chicago road to socialism."[16] Chilean neoliberalism survived this crisis but emerged as a more mixed and pragmatic economic form led by economic thinkers such as Luis Escoba Cerda and Hernán Buchi. This second model was then inherited and to a certain extent continued by the center-left Concertación governments in the 1990s. This later pragmatic turn in the Chilean neoliberal experiment has proven to be the most influential and served as a model for subsequent turns to neoliberalism in other parts of the world (most notably in England under Margaret Thatcher and in the United States under Ronald Reagan).

In much of the economic and political literature on neoliberalism, Chile is named briefly—often in a footnote—as the first experiment in neoliberal reforms.[17] The following study focuses on the Chilean neoliberal experience in an attempt to better understand the profound transformations that this model produced and to map its effects in the realm of cultural production. Although informed by economic and policy approaches, my reading of neoliberalism does not focus on it as a strictly economic field. Rather, following Brett Levinson's reflections on the market, I explore it as "a kind of thinking" and "a way of comprehending the globe."[18] Instead of reproducing a policy-oriented approach to neoliberalism, the following chapters engage with the theoretical underpinnings and most radical ideas produced by the neoliberal movement in order to understand and assess its relation to the cultural expressions associated with it. From a Latin American perspective this demands an exploration of the founding union of authoritarian violence and market freedom upon which Chilean neoliberal modernization is based. This study follows Georg Simmel's insight that a philosophy of money "can only lie on the other side of the economic science of money."[19] In the case of *Speculative Fictions* this insight could be rewritten in the following way:

a theoretical exploration of neoliberalism can only lie on the other side of "actually existing neoliberalism," which nowhere lives up to its own ambitions. This "other side" refers to the ideals and values that neoliberalism has of itself and that for a brief period of Chilean history (the first neoliberal stage) were put into practice.

Neoliberalism and Dedifferentiation

The term *neoliberalism* is dangerously multivalent. Its widespread use, and abuse, as a term that names vastly different economic ideas and historical transformations threatens to render it meaningless. It is sometimes used to describe a full-fledged economic model; other times it is used more loosely to describe a set of economic ideas and policies; and other times it names a specific articulation of culture, politics, and economics in the era of globalization. Rooted in the latter project, I have attempted to curtail some of the term's ambiguities by giving Chilean neoliberalism a specific historical contextualization and periodization. In the following section I develop some of the main theoretical problems that emerge out of the Chilean neoliberal experience.

In his periodization of the concept dedifferentiation, Fredric Jameson pinpoints 1973 as a moment of world crisis (marked by the oil crisis, the end of the gold standard, and the end of traditional communism) when the economic system and the cultural structure of feeling "crystallized."[20] That is to say, the distinction between culture and the economy was eclipsed and collapsed. The term *differentiation* is taken from Niklas Luhmann's work on systems theory and describes the dynamic through which semiautonomous systems emerge out of an undifferentiated mass—such as, for example, social classes, academic disciplines, and professional specializations. *Dedifferentiation,* then, describes a conjuncture when everything including commodity production has become cultural, and culture has become profoundly economic.

Building on the concept of dedifferentiation, *Speculative Fictions* focuses on the cultural effects of neoliberalism's expansion of the economic form so that it applies to the totality of the social sphere, thus eliding any difference between the economic and the social. As Michel Foucault puts it in his work on American neoliberal biopolitics:

"neoliberalism seeks . . . to extend the rationality of the market, the schemes of analysis it proposes, and the decision-making criteria it suggests to areas that are not exclusively or not primarily economic."[21] Thus, economic analytical schemata and the criteria for economic decision making are applied to spheres of life that are not exclusively economic. This represents a transition from trying to govern society in the name of the economy to redefining the social sphere as an economic domain. The economy is no longer considered one social domain among others, but an area that embraces the entirety of human action. As a result, rational economic action becomes the all-encompassing principle of legitimation.

The Chicago School theorist whose work best represents this expansion of the economic field is Nobel Prize–winning economist Gary Becker. One of the axioms that guide Becker's work is that all actors in the social game are rational agents who maximize their advantages in different cost situations. The difference between classical liberalism and Becker's neoliberalism is that the relation between the state and the economy is redefined so that the market becomes the organizing and regulative principle. By encoding the social domain as an economic domain, cost-benefit analysis and market criteria can be applied to all instances of decision making. Thus the notion of natural freedom, which was the ultimate ground of classical liberalism, is replaced by the idea of economic liberty (the entrepreneurial and competitive behavior of economic-rational individuals). This conflation of individual freedoms and liberal democracy with the freedom of the market and of trade—a conflation that has been most powerfully articulated in the work of Friedrich von Hayek—is one of the basic assumptions of the neoliberal project. The contradiction that the Chilean case, the first neoliberal state, brings to light is the seemingly necessary authoritarian nature of such an undertaking. This harkens back to Karl Polanyi's critique of the Mont Pelerin Society and his prediction that ultimately the neoliberal utopian project could only be sustained by resorting to authoritarianism.[22] Giorgio Agamben's critique of Foucault's biopolitical project—which I examine in detail in chapter 4—opens up the discussion of neoliberalism to include its founding moment of authoritarian violence. Agamben's corrective reading of Foucault introduces into the latter's work what Agamben considers a blind spot in regard to the most biopolitical of modern spaces: the concentration camp. In this way a connection is established between a fascist biopolitics (the emergence of *Homo sacer,* which I explore through the Chilean concentration camp *testimonio* and the documentary form) and the neoliberal biopolitical project (the emergence of *Homo economicus,* which I explore through Chilean narrative and visual arts).

Human Capital; or, a Neoliberal Concept of Labor

The Chilean sociologist Manuel Antonio Garretón describes the transition to globalization in Latin America as a move from an industrial society organized around labor and production to a postindustrial society organized around consumption and communication.[23] Garretón is describing what we have called the transition from import-substitution industrialization—which itself is a reaction to the liberal economic policies that led to the depression in the 1930s—to neoliberalism. Import-substitution industrialization, which is characterized by self-sustained growth, an escape from dependence on raw material exports and foreign markets, accelerated industrialization with active government intervention, and the implementation of tariff barriers, is replaced by neoliberal policies, which include lowered trade barriers, an opening to foreign investment, a reduction of the size of the state, the privatization of the public sector, and the market regulation of the economy and of society.[24] Out of this transition *culture* emerges redefined: according to Garretón, it assumes characteristics previously associated with the sphere of politics (and, as was discussed in the previous section, economics). If this is the case, then the question is, what is the fate of labor in a society organized around consumption and communication?

I explore this question by focusing on the neoliberal concept of labor, human capital. Human capital—whose strongest articulation is in the work of Theodore W. Schultz and Gary Becker—refers to the skills that an individual acquires through investments in education, training, social milieu, diet, and hobbies. From the perspective of human capital, life becomes a strategy of self-appreciation where all behavior, action, and decision making is focused on valorizing one's portfolio. Neoliberal subjects become "entrepreneurs of themselves," investors in their own human capital. In the Chilean context, the 1973 document *El ladrillo* served as a blueprint for reorganizing labor around the concept of human capital (I explore the significance of this document more fully in chapters 2 and 6). Couched in the supposedly postideological logic of "eminently technical criteria," this antistatist text's utopic aim is the creation of a world free of centralized planning and bureaucratic direction. It maps out the steps necessary to turn back the tide on four decades of import-substitution industrialization by situating human capital as the central category for Chile's neoliberal project of modernization. An analysis of the narrative fictions produced during this period explore the workings of human capital as a subjective form, and they also reveal an inner homology between two of the dominant ways of conceptualizing labor in our times, immaterial labor and human capital. At stake in both human capital's and immaterial labor's collapsing of the differences between physical and intellectual labor is the place of critique. The blurring of the difference between action and meaning puts into question a critical faculty capable of questioning the meaning of action.

The general architectural assembly of this book is laid out in the following way: it is organized around a central problem, that is, the challenge José Donoso's work passes on to future generations of writers and artists regarding what kind of writing is possible after the epochal transition that 1973 represents. The book's subsequent chapters explore different ways—and different mediums (the novel, documentary film, the *testimonio,* visual arts, and cultural theory)—that the following generation of writers, artists, and thinkers has taken up in order to address Donoso's challenge.

The first chapter connects the tensions between realism and modernism in José Donoso's work to a historical turning point in Chile brought about by the Popular Unity government, the 1973 military coup, and the subsequent neoliberal transition. In so doing, I establish specific interconnections among aesthetic, economic, and political transitions. The novel *Casa de campo* is interpreted as a *transitional* text: its allegorization of the military coup and its turn toward the abstract concepts of political economy (primitive accumulation, commodification, gold, and the move toward to fiduciary currencies) situate Donoso's literary project in relation to a global capitalist transformation, of which the Chilean neoliberal transition has been regarded as a model case. This reading of Donoso's narrative project sets up a challenge for future generations to which all four of the following chapters attempt to respond: how can we understand the cultural forms of neoliberalism?

I follow up with a chapter that explores two ideologically opposed literary representations of Chile's transition from a largely industrial and agrarian order to neoliberal capitalism. In both of the novels—Arturo Fontaine's 1992 *Oír su voz* and Diamela Eltit's 2002 *Mano de obra*—an important shift in the concept of labor is identified and explored. Working from different intellectual traditions—the neoliberal labor concept of human capital and the post-Fordist concept of labor developed by the *operaismo* thinkers (immaterial labor)—the novels reveal a similar inner logic at work in these two increasingly dominant ways of thinking about labor in our times.

The third chapter focuses on the documentary form, a significant cultural force during the dictatorship and postdictatorship periods because of its relation to "the politics of memory." Through an analysis of the work of Patricio Guzmán and Silvio Caiozzi, I map a shift from the vocabulary of collective action and massive mobilizations (the narrative of the Grand March) to a focus on intimate and private stories of tragedy and loss told in a nostalgic and melancholic register. This transformation of the paradigm of memory politics, which was deployed oppositionally during the dictatorship period, is, I argue, connected to the more general neoliberal transformations. The problem of memory and the market, its commodification, informationalization, and mass marketing, is explored in this new market situation in regard to the possibilities of a politics of restitution.

Chapter 4 focuses on Catalina Parra's visual arts project, which engages with the notions of consumption, spending, debt, and the saturation of the image in contemporary culture. Parra's work connects back to the first chapter by explicitly taking up the challenge left by José Donoso's work: how can we begin to understand the cultural forms of neoliberal capitalism? Parra does this by recuperating for the present Donoso's version of the figure of the sewed-up *imbunche* (from the novel *El obsceno pájaro de la noche*). The *imbunche* becomes in Parra's oeuvre a figure for the nightmarish modernity that is driven by the dictatorship and produces sutured, mutilated, and censored bodies in its wake. In this way I trace how one of Donoso's figures is taken up in a moment when it has been intensified and surpassed by the dictatorship, the transition, and the neoliberal condition.

The fifth and concluding chapter further develops the neoliberal concept of labor, human capital, by connecting it to Marx's discussion of the real subsumption of labor under capital. The implications of this connection are explored through a discussion of the role of the intellectual in neoliberal times, the obliteration of the differences between physical and intellectual labor, and Ramón Díaz Eterovic's detective novel *A la sombra del dinero.* The chapter finishes with an overview of the project of *Speculative Fictions.*

1

THE BROODER'S STARTLED GAZE

José Donoso, Broken Allegories, and the Commodity Form

The brooder whose startled gaze falls on the fragment in his hand becomes an allegorist.
—Walter Benjamin, "Central Park"

According to the poet Pablo Neruda, José Donoso was destined to write "the great Chilean social novel."[1] Yet instead of being recognized as the Chilean Balzac, Donoso has perhaps become best known for his literary project's modernist disarticulation of the very possibility of a realist novel capable of accessing a vision of totality. This focus on his modernist approach is based on a partial analysis of Donoso's work, privileging his formally experimental novels such as *El obsceno pájaro de la noche* and *Taratuta; Naturaleza muerta con cachimba* over more realist-oriented work such as *Coronación, Este domingo,* and *El lugar sin límites.* This chapter does not attempt to claim Donoso for one faction or the other. Rather, it works toward a reformulation of the question regarding whether Donoso is really a Lukacsian realist whose novels "reflect" the unity of economics and ideology as an objective whole (the ever-elusive concept of totality) or, on the contrary, whether he achieves a high modernist vision, tearing heterogeneous bits of reality away from their social contexts and juxtaposing them in order to produce subjectivist narratives. The argument advanced is that it is the unrelenting tension—and ultimate crisis—of these two aesthetic and cognitive forms (realism and modernism) in Donoso's work that makes him so valuable for understanding the historical transformations brought upon by the Chilean neoliberal transition. The crisis of these two forms coincides with a historical turning point in Chile, the 1970s transition from one regime of accumulation (an industrial and traditionally agrarian order based on labor and production) to another (neoliberal capitalism based on consumption and communication). Focusing on the change in Donoso's literary project as he passes from *El obsceno pájaro de la noche* to *Casa de campo,* and against the dismissal of his apocalyptic tones as merely symptoms of bourgeois decadence, I explore how his work identifies a crisis in allegory's function as a transitional form and then struggles to articulate what kind of writing is possible after the military coup.

Since his earliest writings Donoso has expressed an ambiguous and at times capricious relation with the different variants of the Latin American realist tradition. He has explicitly rejected the *criollista* novel's mimetic realism, its exclusive concern for the rural (understood as a nostalgia for an agrarian past in an era of immigration and economic expansion), and its search for an autochthonous literary expression. This position vis-á-vis a certain form of the Latin American realist novel would seem to situate Donoso firmly within the Latin American literary boom's cosmopolitan aesthetic project; it reinforces the boom's parricidal tabula rasa myth and the claim that the preceding realist narrative project had been devoured by a descriptive and documentary passion for nature. Yet two immediate problems result from this positioning of Donoso within the modernist boom project—this approach cannot account for the entirety of his literary production (including some of his best work, such as *El lugar sin límites*), nor can it go beyond the cliché that conceives the rich and varied tradition of Latin American realism in terms that are too mimetic, too rural, and too local.

Donoso's novels represent a continuation—however contentious—of the critical-realist tradition rather than its rupture. Because of the split in the critical reception of his work, his novels have been read both as a notable expression of realist narrative and as marking a seemingly radical break with it (*El obsceno pájaro de la noche* is generally considered the paradigmatic example). Realist readings of

Donoso's realist novels emphasize his description of the fragile and decadent upper crust of Chilean society with a language that is richly local and transparent (as in the work of critics Hugo Achugar, Hernán Vidal, and Antonio Cornejo Polar), whereas modernist perspectives emphasize Donoso's radical signifying strategies, subversive and experimental attitude toward social institutions and language, and refusal of totalizing narratives (as in the work of Philip Swanson, Sharon Magnarelli, Ana Dopico, and Adriana Valdés, among others). The question then is—how do we understand or resolve this realist/modernist tension that has polarized the reception of Donoso's work? Can it be simply explained as a progressive change in his writing and aesthetic project? Is there an early realist Donoso versus a late modernist Donoso? Alternatively, I will argue that the dyad is a constant and productive tension throughout his work, one that will reach both its pinnacle and its ultimate limit in the 1978 novel *Casa de campo,* which, not uncoincidentally, allegorizes the Chilean Popular Unity government and the 1973 military coup.

Casa de campo's narrator presents a critique of realism that also attempts to give an account of the modernist literary aesthetic that supersedes it. The narrator begins by explaining the intrusive commentaries that are strewn throughout the novel: they are meant to reveal the artifice and manipulation behind the storytelling by creating a distance between the reader and the material of the novel. As the narrator informs us: "I do it with the modest end of proposing that the public accept what I write as artifice."[2] By actively maintaining this distance, the novel interrupts and frustrates the reader's identification with the narrative. The "modest end" alluded to here is the undermining of traditional mimetic representational categories, accomplished through the implementation of a version of Bertolt Brecht's estrangement effect. As *Casa de campo*'s narrator continues to elaborate on literary strategies, the novel's complicated relation to the realism/modernism problem begins to reveal itself. The narrator explains that his constant interruptions correspond to discredited and old-fashioned narrative machinery, which is considered to be just as substantial as more modern conventions that masquerade as "good taste."[3] What, precisely, are the "discredited and old-fashioned" narrative machines that the narrator is referring to here? Is this a move toward reclaiming the much-disparaged realist novel? If so, then this seems to fly in the face of the boom's parricidal strategy of proclaiming a new beginning with no literary fathers. And if this is indeed the case, then how does one understand the reference to overcoming "conventions that masquerade as 'good taste'"? "Good taste," a category charged with classist inflections, is hardly an accurate characterization of the dominant representational strategies associated with the Latin American literary boom.

The literary criticism on Donoso that has picked up on this shift has read the above passage as a straightforward call for a return to realist representational strategies. In *Casa de campo*'s case, this implies a return to that realist stalwart, authorial omniscience, and a seeming abandonment of some of the most characteristic boom strategies so provocatively deployed in *El obsceno pájaro de la noche:* metalanguage, the distortion of time and space, and a concern with formal experimentation. Yet there is a problem with this reading of Donoso: authorial intervention is so exaggerated in *Casa de campo* that it exceeds, and even becomes intolerable to, a realistic narrative. To be clear, there is no contradiction between authorial intervention and realism, but the exaggerated degree to which *Casa de campo* pushes the figure moves it beyond the conventions of traditional realism. The novel in fact exemplifies many of those supposedly abandoned boom attributes noted above, which no one would confuse with "good taste." I propose that its narrator's call for a return to "old-fashioned narrative machinery now in discredit" is already a return to the modernist boom novel that by the mid-1970s was the target of attack by a younger generation of writers.[4] For Donoso this return is a necessary part of a project that attempts to reinvent a form of realism, while at the same time incorporating modernism's violent renewal of perceptions. Such a project would involve, simultaneously, a critique of the modernist innovation fetish (which is already an exhausted literary project at the time Donoso is writing *Casa de campo*), a revamping of modernist forms, and an exploration of what new forms of realism might look like. The return, therefore, is a way of thinking about future realisms.

The Geopolitics of the Realism/Modernism Debate

The groundwork needed for the development of a response to the problems described above requires a reengagement with the realism/modernism debate.[5] Donoso's literary project complicates any attempt to reduce the tensions between realism and modernism to a simple taking of sides, and it deploys a powerful critique of homogeneous, unilinear, and developmentalist theories of the realism/modernism dynamic. For example, David Harvey's *The Condition of Postmodernity* puts forward a developmentalist periodization of the realism/modernism dynamic. Paradoxically this periodization is deployed in order to elaborate a "radical readjustment in the sense of time and space in economic, political, and cultural life."[6] Harvey sketches out a series of economic and political crises that took place in Europe in 1846–47 (the crisis of capitalist overaccumulation, the internationalization of money power, the tension between credit and species money, political turmoil and revolutionary movements) that, he argues, led to a crisis of realist representation. It is out of this realist crisis that modernism emerges. The "death" of literary realism is understood by its supposed inability to represent modernity's increasing spatial simultaneity.[7] When it is presented in this simplified and conventional form, realism functions as a contrast to modernism's more complex representational strategies (symbolism, expressionism, cubism, constuctivism, surrealism, etc.). The dyad is then too neatly grafted onto a historical period that is understood to be realist pre-1846–47 and modernist post-1846–47. In contrast, a more complex notion of the realist form as a sensuous model of writing about the properties of things that is committed to understanding and describing real social processes reveals a cognitive project capable of accessing the forces of transformation in a specific moment in history. The continuation of realism beyond 1846–47, its formal adaptability, and its continued importance call into question the developmentalist conceptualization of the relation between realism and modernism. The shortcomings of this kind of conceptualization become even more evident when considered in relation to a twentieth-century writer like Donoso, where what is needed is a differential notion of temporality, in which periods are both discontinuous from each other and simultaneously heterogeneous within themselves. Donoso's call for a return to "old-fashioned narrative machinery now in discredit" denies that there is a radical break between realism and modernism; it challenges us to conceptualize realism as a kind of modernism in its own right.

Fredric Jameson's work on this subject comes closest to theorizing Donoso's articulation of realism/modernism. For Jameson, realism contains within itself many of the qualities usually associated with modernism: it is subversive, critical, destructive, and it clears away the useless and jumbled monumentality of older cultural forms.[8] Realism does this by seizing on the properties, subjectivities, institutions, and forms of an older precapitalist life world and stripping them of their hierarchical and religious content. Therefore modernism is not so much an overcoming of realism, but an intensification of the processes of reification already at work in realism. The modernist difference is that these processes are intensified to such a point that they end up cannibalizing the realist form. The basic ideological preconditions of realism, such as the belief in a stable social reality, are unmasked, demystified, and ultimately discredited by modernism. In this way, Jameson puts the realism/modernism debate within the broader context of a transition from one mode of production to another while stressing that these transitional moments are themselves always part of a permanent struggle between coexisting modes of production.

This understanding of the relation between modernism and realism as an intensification of the work of reification moves us beyond the developmentalist view critiqued above and approaches an understanding of what is actually going on in Donoso's literary project. The work that still needs to be done is to decenter geopolitically the predominately European trajectory of the realism/modernism debate and think it from a Latin American context. Perry Anderson's critique of Marshall Berman's conceptualization of modernism is a step in this direction; it introduces into the discussion the centrality of Third World modernism. Regarding Berman's now-classic book *All That Is Solid Melts into Air,* Anderson points out the following: "It is significant that so many of Berman's examples of what he reckons to be the great modernist achievements of our time should be taken from Latin American literature. For in the Third World generally, a kind of shadow configuration of what once prevailed in the First World does exist today."[9] Anderson's conjunctural reading of modernism opposes what he refers to as Berman's perennial modernism—modernism as the abstract expression of a dynamic and eternal process of modernization—with a historically grounded version. Thus the "shadow configuration" refers to the necessary historical conditions out of which a modernist poetics can emerge. These conditions are summarized as three coordinates: (1) the persistence in some form of the "anciens régimes," (2) the emergence of key technologies of the second industrial revolution, and (3) the proximity of social revolution. In Europe and North America, Anderson argues, these historical conditions disappear after the Second World War through the universalization of bourgeois democracy and the massification of Fordism. It is the continuation of these coordinates in the Third World that gives rise to its modernist production:

> Pre-capitalist oligarchies of various kinds, mostly of a landowning character, abound; capitalist development is typically far more rapid and dynamic, where it does occur, in these regions than in the metropolitan zones, but on the other hand is infinitely less stabilized or consolidated; social revolution haunts these societies as a permanent possibility, one indeed already realized in countries close to home—Cuba or Nicaragua, Angola or Vietnam. These are the conditions that have produced the genuine masterpieces of recent years that conform to Berman's categories: Gabriel García Márquez's *One Hundred Years of Solitude,* or Salman Rushdie's *Midnight's Children,* from Colombia or India, or films like Yilmiz Güney's *Yol* from Turkey.[10]

Opposed to Berman's timeless conception of modernism, Anderson diagrams a society at a specific historical crossroads. The question then is—does Donoso's literary project situate itself within this specific historical crossroads? Likewise, does Anderson's triangulation of Third World modernism offer insights into Donoso's articulation of the realism/modernism dynamic? Perhaps, but with the important caveat that it can only really be applied to Donoso's work up until the 1968 publication of *El obsceno pájaro de la noche. Casa de campo,* which was published in 1978, marks a transition from the historical crossroads to which Anderson alludes. In the Chilean case, and specifically in regard to Donoso's modernism, the historical crossroads mentioned above has been, at an accelerated rate, left behind. That is to say, the coordinates that in Anderson's diagram triangulate modernism as a cultural field—the presence of an aristocratic or landowning class against which modernist forms can measure themselves, the incipient and novel emergence of communicative technologies, and the empowering specter of social revolution—have either been destroyed or effectively run their course by, respectively, the 1967 agrarian reform, the rapid massification of television after the 1960s World Cup, and the 1973 military coup.

It is not by chance that *Casa de campo* coincides with an epochal turning point in Chile: the transition from one regime of accumulation to another and the transformation of Chile into one of the modern laboratories of neoliberal economic experimentation. Donoso's novel corresponds to a different historical crossroads from the Third World modernism described by Anderson—one where modernist representation has already done the work of clearing away older representational forms in order to make way for new experimental rhetorical instruments and fictional laboratories. It is from this uncharted space that Donoso's call for a return to "old-fashioned narrative machinery now in discredit" needs to be understood.

To frame the geopolitics of the realism/modernism debate from a Latin American perspective, I want to compare Donoso's literary project with Antonio Cornejo Polar's theoretical project of Latin American literary heterogeneity. The Peruvian literary critic is one of the best readers of Donoso's early literary trajectory; his chief assertion is that Donoso's literary project is more apocalyptic than foundational. Mapping Donoso's work from *Coronación* (1956) to *El obsceno pájaro de la noche* (1968), Cornejo Polar inventories the growing intensification of apocalyptic elements in these novels and highlights two: the destruction of history and the crisis of the principle of identity. The idea is that in Donoso's novels, history—understood by Cornejo Polar as a dialectical process of oppositions—is annulled: "Whether it is because nothing changes, or because everything repeats itself, once again, spinning in a never ending circle, history becomes impossible."[11] Similarly with identity, Cornejo Polar notes in these novels a dilution of characters as receptacles of a consistent individuality. Focusing on *El obsceno pá-*

jaro de la noche as the most extreme limit to which Donoso takes this apocalyptic project, Cornejo Polar pronounces that "it [the novel] is a cruel simulacrum that appears to create when it is really destroying."[12] His principle objection is that Donoso narrates the degradation of a local *criollo* bourgeois society and passes it off as the representation of a universal ontological destruction. Cornejo Polar condemns this as a false universality, one that is constitutive of Donoso's literary project. In a gesture that mimics the boom's own parricidal fixations, Cornejo Polar ends his essay with a call to the new generation of writers to abandon Donoso's apocalyptic narrative project and to dedicate themselves to the urgent task of recuperating the meaning and experience of history.

Three years later, in his foundational essay on heterogeneous literatures, Cornejo Polar returns to Donoso in order to develop his argument that "literatures that are subject to a double sociocultural statute" (which refers principally to Andean *indigenismo* but also includes New World chronicles, *gauchesca* literature, *negrismo,* and *lo real maravilloso*) are privileged texts from which to develop a project of literary criticism that is "truly Latin American." One of the challenges with which Cornejo Polar is faced in order to advance his thesis on heterogeneous literatures is how to distinguish them from homogeneous literature.[13] In order to establish this distinction, Donoso is key. Donoso becomes, for Cornejo Polar, the prototypical exponent of "a society that talks to itself."[14] That is to say, Donoso expresses bourgeois perspectives using bourgeois narrative techniques that circulate among bourgeois readers. Cornejo Polar repeats his earlier critique of illegitimate universality in Donoso, claiming that the only possible outside to this bourgeois space permitted in these novels is an ideological move that totalizes what is exclusive to one particular social group. Thus, according to Cornejo Polar, the closed and suffocating bourgeois spaces (houses mainly) that proliferate in Donoso's novels do not allow the oxygen to breathe that the vibrant dialectical space of a literature defined by a plurality of sociocultural signs does. José María Arguedas is taken up as the paradigmatic figure of this other, more heterogeneous literature. Hence, for Cornejo Polar, in order to found a new Latin American narrative based on the concept of heterogeneity, it is necessary to abandon the apocalyptic strains he finds in Donoso, which do not allow the dialectical leap necessary to pass from destruction to construction of a different and better system.

Cornejo Polar's revelation that there is a steady intensification of apocalyptic elements in Donoso's novels is, I believe, an accurate and important insight. Where I differ with his reading is in regard to the assessment that this apocalyptic intensification implies an ontologized notion of decadence. The destructive elements in Donoso reveal more than simply the degradation of a local *criollo* elite. And in this respect there are obvious parallels between Cornejo Polar's critique of Donoso and Lukács's more general critique of modernism. Both repeat the same claim that the decadence of a particular class is given an ontological status, and both signal the negation of history and the disintegration of identity as the defining characteristics of their respective objects of study.[15] By reductively equating Donoso's work with a single social class (the bourgeoisie), Cornejo Polar reproduces one of the problems found in much of Lukács's work. A consequence of this is that Cornejo Polar's theory of Latin American heterogeneity is unable to take into account a transvestite figure like La Manuela, of *El lugar sin límites,* in a more complex way than as just another example of local bourgeois decadence.[16]

If we decide not to heed Cornejo Polar's plea to abandon Donoso's literary project, the question then becomes, what is actually at stake in this apocalyptic intensification? The answer to this lies in the combination of two premises: (1) the conceptualization—developed in the previous section—of realism and modernism as cultural forms in the service of a larger project of intensifying capitalist reification, and (2) the idea that by the early 1970s the specific historical crossroads for Third World modernism (the triangulation of coordinates developed by Perry Anderson) had been effectively left behind. The work of seizing and reifying older forms, properties, subjectivities, and institutions that had been previously deployed by both realism and modernism was, in this transitional period, reaxiomatized according to an emerging neoliberal logic of accumulation. Thus Antonio Cornejo Polar's apostolic call for a return to history as a dialectical process of oppositions and the need to return to a stable notion of identity could be understood as a rejection of the epochal transition being foretold in Donoso's work. Donoso's literary project is not a retreat from the meaning and experience of history, but an inquiry into what this meaning and experience might look like after the military coup, after the exhaustion of the Latin American boom's modernist project, and at the beginnings of the neoliberal transition. To put it more specifically, it is the Chilean neoliberal transition that constitutes the delimited constellation out of which Donoso's specific reconfiguration of the realism/modernism dynamic—marked by the passage from *El obsceno pájaro de la noche* to *Casa de campo*—reveals itself. One possible reading of what the narrative move in *Casa de campo* represents in regard to Donoso's literary trajectory and, more generally, in regard to the articulation of realism and modernism in contemporary Latin American literature is that the novel proposes a resuscitation of realism as a possible renewal of an exhausted modernist aesthetic. In a moment when the culture industry has become all pervasive, what once seemed experimental in modernism has become the dominant style of commodity production.

And yet this does not tell the whole story, for modernism and realism do not appear as clearly definable or independent unities that occur in succession or stages in Donoso's literary trajectory. Elements of both coexist within the same narrative texts. How do we understand this specific articulation of realism and modernism? What historical conjuncture gave rise to it? As I stated earlier, Donoso's call for a return to "old-fashioned narrative machinery now in discredit" is not an attempt to revive an older experience of social life associated with realism (secularization, a particular nineteenth-century experience of the city, and an interest in the physical properties of things). *Casa de campo,* with its strong emphasis on referential interruption, is by its own admission "totally alien" to the mimetic criteria of art; at every step there is an insistence that old-style realism, as seductive as it might be, is irretrievably a thing of the past.[17] Donoso's is a return to realism that is fully aware of its limitations.

The forms of abstraction that begin to emerge in *Casa de campo* are of a different order than those associated with earlier realist narratives or modernist boom aesthetics. They are forms of abstraction marked by the emergence of economic ideas that begin to usurp the roles of characters, figures, and themes. This is in part what defines Donoso's novel as a *transitional* text: there is a tendency toward the abstract concepts of political economy (primitive accumulation, commodification, exchange value, gold and the turn to fiduciary currencies, and finance capital). By *transitional text* I mean a text that emerges in a moment of crisis—representational, political, economic—and engages in a struggle for a language in order to name the emergent formation. The following three sections of this essay develop the emergence of these economic figures in *Casa de campo* and place Donoso's literary transition in relation to a global capitalist transformation, of which the Chilean neoliberal transition has been regarded as a model case.

Casa de campo's Secret of Primitive Accumulation

Casa de campo's allegorization of the Chilean Popular Unity period, the military coup, and the neoliberal transition begins with a reflection on what Karl Marx calls the history of economic original sin: primitive accumulation. This is capital's prehistory, the necessary starting point that makes possible the movement of capital accumulation by producing a surplus value from a previous precapitalist production process. "So-called primitive accumulation" is what Marx condemns as a moral fairytale about the originary split between the diligent and the lazy, which traditional political economy developed to explain why capitalists and workers exist.[18] As Althusser and Balibar have noted, what is of particular interest about Marx's discussion on this topic is the revelation that this separation can never be adequately explained from within the logic of capitalist accumulation because it necessarily presupposes existing capital in order to accumulate capital: "The production of this original capital therefore constitutes a threshold and crossing this threshold cannot be explained by the action of the law of capitalist accumulation alone."[19] Paradoxically, primitive accumulation is an origin that lies outside of capitalism.

In the novel, the mythic foundation of Marulanda and the Venturas' country house is—as stories of primitive accumulation always are—about conquest, enslavement, robbery, and murder. The civilizing mission of the first Venturas to arrive in Marulanda is a war against the so-called cannibals. This war resulted in the capture of land and mines and the transformation of the natives into labor (driven off their land, they are turned into vegetarians, their history is forgotten, and their arms are taken away and used to make the fence that separates them from the Venturas' estate). The natives are put to work in the mountain gold mines, the source of the Venturas' wealth, hammering the gold into thin laminate sheets that are then exported to the opulent centers of the world.

The work of primitive accumulation is completed by the foreign thistle plants (*gramíneas*) that were introduced by the Venturas. These plants, whose growth parallels the expansion of capital in the region, were meant to produce an agricultural base even more profitable than the mines, but after a few years they choked out the native vegetation and took over the plains. The thistles turned out to be economically useless but fundamental to the Venturas' well-being: the plants were so aggressively invasive that they drove all of the natives off the plains, forcing them to relocate to the mountains, where they were incorporated into the mines as workers in the gold-production process.

In the telling of this story of capitalist origins, *Casa de campo* accounts for the two constitutive acts that, according to Marx, define primitive accumulation. First, the expropriation that precedes the capitalist production process is described in the second part of the novel. This expropriation divorces the producer from the means of production and establishes what Marx describes as the fundamental division between the great majority who despite all their labor have nothing to sell but themselves (in this case the natives) and the wealth of the few who have long ceased to work (the Venturas). The second act of primitive accumulation is the bloody legislation that follows the expropriation: a regime of penalization and torture that produces "bird free" workers.

Thus Donoso commences his allegorical reflections on Popular Unity, the 1973 military coup, and the Chilean neoliberal transition with this well-known story of the discovery of gold and silver in the Americas and the subsequent extirpation, enslavement, and entombment of the indigenous population. By beginning with this history of primitive accumulation, *Casa de campo* not only frames the novel around one of the fundamental concepts of political economy but mirrors a historical process that John Kraniauskas has called "ongoing primitive accumulation." Primitive accumulation doesn't merely precede capitalism but continually accompanies it. As a result, both modernization and the violence pertaining to the 1973 military coup appear in the novel as an uninterrupted process of primitive accumulation.

Gold, the Hoarder, and Finance Capital

As the novel's story of primitive accumulation explains, the Venturas' social standing and fortune are based on their monopoly of gold mining in the area. For this reason the origins of their downfall precede the adults' fateful trip away from the country house, which in turn unleashes the children's revolutionary energy. It begins with the gold-bundle number 48779/TA64: the first faulty gold bundle. This gold bundle, improperly made, is passed off as a proper one by one of the natives, Pedro Crisólogo, and sits in the Venturas' vault, slowly deteriorating. Hermógenes Ventura, who is in charge of the Venturas' gold-trade accounts, sees it as the beginning of the end. It is, he claims, an act of sedition and rebellion that reveals the corrupting influence of foreigners over the Venturas' supposedly docile natives (ironically the corrupting influence turns out to be one of their own, Malvina—the outcast and illegitimate cousin who, having no legal claim to the Venturas' wealth, steals and buries their money). The faulty gold bundle is a harbinger of the crisis to come because through its imperfections it breaks the illusion of an economic empire that goes back generations and is solidly supported by vast and perfectly crafted gold reserves.

Of the emancipatory projects the novel uses to allegorize the divisions and revolutionary ferment of the Popular Unity period, the one that will have the most far-reaching consequences is Hermógenes Ventura's daughter Casilda's project to steal the gold reserves. For Casilda, the other projects in gestation (her cousin Mauro's spears project and her cousin Wenceslao's attempts to free his father, Adriano Gomara/Salvador Allende) offer only the illusion of liberty. The only real liberty, she believes, can come from possessing the gold. In contrast to these other more euphoric projects, Casilda's is a joyless undertaking, void of any affect, love, or revolutionary exuberance: "for these two [Casilda and her cousin Fabio, whom she enlists] the party had never existed. It wasn't that their obsession had changed their behavior: they were dry, pure structure, pure design."[20] For Casilda, stealing the gold holds no collective or utopian promise. Unlike the other projects that emerge when the adults leave, not only does the gold heist not involve the other cousins, but it reveals her resistance to joining them and, what is more, her disinterest in leading them. Instead of either sovereignty or the articulation of an alternative social model, what Casilda wants is "to shatter, to demolish her father's world, so that her hatred might finally be rid of its object and, rendered pointless, stop hurting her."[21] The gold heist is a cruel simulacra that is more destructive than foundational.

What is at the root of Casilda's hatred? How does stealing the gold render it pointless? Casilda knows more about the gold than anyone else, but hers is only an abstract knowledge. She has never actually seen or touched it. The bundles of gold sheets that the natives bring are always wrapped in thistle leaves. She is permitted to know gold only as an abstraction, not as an actual substance. Transformed into the accountant and bookkeeper of the Venturas' gold, Casilda is the only one, apart from her father, "who knows the exact quantities, weights, values, production, and availability of the metal that enriched the family."[22] Casilda shares her father's secret: the book of fraudulent accounts that reveals the amount that Hermógenes was skimming off the Venturas' earnings. She is complicit with her father's secret (and this is the strong bond that unites them), but what she really resents is being deprived of the materiality of the gold. Casilda suspects that her father's greatest deception and his unforgivable betrayal is having her believe that the gold has no inherent value: "She wasn't satisfied with his efforts to convince her that the gold was simply an idea that figured in ledgers and transactions, that only when it was sold, traded, exported, put in savings, transformed into stocks and bonds, into loans and mortgages, did it acquire value; and that to the contrary it had none in and of itself, as the sacrosanct substance she was forbidden to see."[23] She resists the notion that her figures and calculations have anything to do with the "sacrosanct essence of the gold." These attitudes correspond to the classic definition of the hoarder. Casilda eschews the circulation of commodities, the alternating flow of buying and selling, and retreats into the hoarding of money in its gold form. For Marx, the hoarder impulse corresponds to "the passionate desire to hold fast to the product of the first metamorphosis," and that product is the "transformed shape of the commodity, or its gold chrysalis."[24] What this means is that circulation's *perpetuum mobile,* which for Casilda is associated with her accounting manipulations (selling, trading, exporting, and investing the gold), needs to be arrested in order to reconnect with Marx's notion of gold as a glittering incarnation of modern society's innermost principle of life. By removing gold from circulation, the hoarder preserves its quasi-mystical status as commodity-cum-exchange value. Buried or hoarded, gold money preserves its quality of being a social form of wealth that is always ready to be used and as the radical leveler of all commodities. Casilda the hoarder seeks to possess the gold as money because she derives no enjoyment from the selling, purchasing, or exchanging of commodities. Her enjoyment comes from preserving gold money as a fetish object. Gold money becomes her aesthetic religion. This explains the joylessness of her undertaking, for the hoarder works through abstinence—she gives up the lusts of her flesh (the enjoyment associated with the buying and selling of commodities) in order to isolate a fetish object, gold money.

Yet Casilda's relationship to the gold cannot be fully explained by Marx's description of the gold hoarder. She is clearly not a naive hoarder nor someone who considers value to be inseparable from the value form (where, e.g., gold *is* value and not just its representation). For the naive hoarder, whom Marx identifies as the Western European peasant and the barbarian, an increase in an amount of gold is equivalent to an increase in value. Casilda's anxiety about dematerialization needs to be understood as a symptom of a larger economic crisis that developed after Marx's analysis of the hoarder: the passage from metallic to fiduciary forms of money. According to the economic historian Randall Hinshaw, this transformation took place between 1937, when commodity money (gold) made up 91 percent of the world's monetary reserves, and 1966, when this figure dropped down to 49 percent.[25] Narrowing this transformation down even further, Milton Friedman claims that 1971 marks a revolutionary change in economic history: all currencies become fiduciary monies, and international trade and exchange eliminate any reference to metals.[26] Before this date, paper money is resorted to mainly in times of crisis such as war, but 1971 ushers in the age of dematerialized currency, and from then on it becomes the normal state of affairs. The point is that however it is evaluated, the periodization of the passage from metallic to fiduciary forms of money corresponds to the period being allegorized in Donoso's novel, and more specifically, it corresponds to Casilda's relation to the gold. If, as I described earlier, one of the qualities of nineteenth- and early twentieth-century literary realism is its representation of the new social relations that began emerging around a newfound interest in the physical and sensory properties of objects, then Casilda's desire for the sensory materiality of the gold can be understood as a nostalgic desire for a return to this kind of realist representation and the social relations it engendered in the face of the rapid transformations being produced by a new age of dematerialized currency. By stealing the gold from the Venturas' vault and removing it from circulation, Casilda wishes to restitute gold as the holy grail of the money form; she wishes to restitute its "sacrosanct essence."

Exploring the relation between the crisis of realism in the late nineteenth-century novel and the end of gold money, Jean-Joseph Goux's *The Coiners of Language* concludes that the two events are part and parcel of the same crisis. It is a crisis of money and language that ruptures the relation between sign and thing, undermines representation, and ushers in the age of the floating signifier. Goux sees in André Gide's novel *The Counterfeiters* the central metaphor for calling into question the role of general equivalents. For Goux this includes all values that regulate exchange: gold, the father, language, and the phallus. These are structurally homogeneous general equivalents that function in terms of measurement and exchange. Their crisis is also the crisis of the novel as a genre. This crisis is marked by a shift from legitimation by representation (a standard or treasury that offers a guarantee of a transcendental signifier or referent) to the convertibility of signifiers (they become empty tokens in a process of infinite slippage). This historical turning point or transition from a "gold language" to a "token language" is grafted, by Goux, onto the passage from the nineteenth-century realist novels of Hugo, Zola, and Balzác to the modernist sensibilities of Gide, Mallarmé, and Valéry. *Casa de campo* both revisits the gold-standard/realist-novel fracture described by Jean-Joseph Goux and reveals it to have always been based on a sleight of hand.[27] In her quest to possess the material essence of the gold, Casilda discovers that like any money form, gold is always abstract. Its value is never intrinsic but is always to be found outside of its materiality in the speculative mediations that she herself performed (calculations, measures, and transactions). The scene in the novel when the cousins finally break into the vault where the gold reserves are kept depicts an orgiastic encounter between Casilda and the mystic materiality of the gold that she has for so long desired. When she finally breaks open one of the gold-sheet bundles—it is not coincidental that it is the faulty bundle 48779/TA64—and scatters the gold particles and dust all over her body, her dreams seem realized: "She pawed the powdered gold, staining her arms as if with yellow blood, her hands, wrists, and fingernails glinting, her face metallic, her hair like golden foam. Crushed metal particles flew up from her bloody hands, her lashes gold, her eyebrows gold, the grimace of her childish smile frozen into a timeless mask of hatred."[28]

For Casilda the hoarder, gold is money itself, not its representation. Her desire goes beyond simply an instrumental or economic interest in gold. Her attraction is to its very materiality, to its glitter and its feel. She is attracted to those values that lie beyond the quantitative computations of gold at which she is so proficient. This attempt to ground the economic in the aesthetic as a way of fixing the value of gold is undermined in the novel. Casilda's desire for the materiality of gold turns out to be as arbitrary as any of the economic values with which it is endowed. In the end, far from returning her to a state of plenitude, the project of stealing the gold ends up demystifying the realist illusion of a transcendental signifier or referent. It ends up eliminating the possibility of any kind of straightforward return to a world of "gold language." This is why the orgiastic scene of bodily connection with the materiality of the gold is necessarily so fleeting. It is a turning point where Casilda realizes that the only way to replace the previous owner of the gold, her father, is to be "ruthless before the seduction of the moment" and reintroduce the gold into the flow of circulation for her own benefit.

Despite the failed attempt to reconnect with the materiality of the gold, Casilda in a sense achieves the task she had initially proposed of demolishing her father's world. It turns out that Casilda's role in this is only to initiate the process: after breaking into the vault, she cannot transport it. At this point the gold is hijacked by her cousin Malvina, who has established a pact with a group of outlaw natives and has been developing contacts with gold exporters in the city. In this way the gold flows out of Marulanda, revealing how the seemingly impenetrable barriers that protected the Venturas and their gold (the massive fence made from the natives' own spears, the giant locked gates, the vault, the thistle-covered plains, and the mountains) were all an illusion that easily falls away under the wings of the gold's flight. What is ultimately revealed by the gold heist is the mutually accepted but hidden fictionality of commodity money. The Venturas' vast gold reserves maintained the appearance that monetary signs represent physical realities by holding large quantities of gold to back up monetary reference. In other words, the Venturas' wealth, privilege, and status are contingent on maintaining the illusion of a gold bedrock.

On the return from their trip, the adult Venturas find the country house in chaos, their children in revolt, the mines abandoned, their gold reserves stolen, and their monopoly in jeopardy. The violent and bloody assault on the country home carried out by the servants, armed and commissioned by the adult Venturas, is ordered as a last-ditch effort to restore the old order. But with the passing away of the illusion of a gold standard, it is an order beyond restoration, and the Venturas, conscious of this, plan to sell it all—the house, the plains, and the mines—to foreign investors. Considering the chaotic state of things, the foreign investors are hoping to get everything at a greatly reduced price, but the Venturas think otherwise and are counting on the servants to keep things in martial order and maintain the illusion that nothing has changed.

The novel allegorizes the 1973 military coup as an epochal changing of the guard from the hegemony of the Venturas to the hegemony of finance capital (represented by the foreign investors). The Venturas' dramatic loss of cultural capital is put on display during the negotiations with the foreign investors. The Venturas assume the role of petitioners and soon face a humiliating social situation where they realize that what were once their greatest assets, their name and class status, no longer mean anything. The scene reveals that "what they *were* lacked any value in the foreigner's eyes."[29] The negotiations are marked by a stark contrast between the pretentious, lyrical, and hyperbolic language with which the Venturas describe their world and the clear, precise, and pragmatic language of the foreign investors. The Venturas' quaint but obsolescent *preciosista* (precious or affected) language conforms to the commandment that nothing should be confronted openly—it understands life as pure allusion, ritual, and symbol. The end of the Venturas' reign also marks the end of the literary rhetoric associated with this oligarchic class. The foreign investors are the harbingers of a new realism: against the Venturas' subjectivism and ornate *preciosismo,* the investors' narrative is parse, practical, and factitious. Under the scrutiny of the foreign investors' neorealist perspective, all the Venturas' illusions begin to fall: their extensive land holdings turn out to be just a small park, their illustrious country mansion a half-ruined cottage, the idyllic waterfall retreat a blind woman's fantasy, the supposedly docile natives cannibals, the masked Ventura children tortured. As one of the foreign investors informs the Venturas: "The subjectivity that colors your judgment of everything pertaining to the family is at total odds with reality seen from outside and from another perspective."[30] This other perspective is a pragmatic one that proves to be impervious to the Venturas' lyrical seductions and ends up establishing a brutally realist order of things. The realist discourse of the foreign investors is the discourse of finance capital. It proposes an intensification of the processes of primitive accumulation that founded the Venturas' estate. This begins by the elimination—through mechanization—of what has been the productive backbone of the Ventura's gold empire, the native workforce. Within the allegorical logic of the novel, the natives represent the proletariat, so what is being suggested by the foreign investors is the elimination of people from the productive process. These changes signal the end of the Venturas' monopoly capitalism, the transition from one regime of accumulation to another, and the increasing dominance of the abstract and speculative logic of finance capitalism.

Broken Allegories and the Commodity Form

The reader of José Donoso's *Casa de campo* is presented with the seductive game of trying to identify all of the novel's many allegorical references to the Chilean Popular Unity period and the 1973 military coup. One of the pitfalls of this kind of reading—although it is on a basic level still a necessary exercise—is to reinforce the Romantic aesthetic tradition of privileging the symbol over the allegory.[31] Hans-Georg Gadamer continues this tradition and expresses his disdain for allegory with the claim that when all the equivalencies have been established, allegory is left emptied of any signifying potential (opposed to the symbol, which is infinitely suggestive). Thus for Gadamer, symbol and allegory are opposed to each other in the same way that "art is opposed to non-art."[32] The most brutally Gadamerian critique of *Casa de campo* was written in 1979 by the conservative literary critic Ignacio Valente:

> The allegory is obvious. The Ventura lineage is the dominant class. The servants are the military, the natives the proletariat, the myth of anthropophagi is international communism. Uncle Adriano has points of contact with Allende, the entrance of the natives into the mansion signifies the triumph of Popular Unity, the following chaos is its three-year rule, the victory of the servants represents September 11th; the butler relates to general Pinochet, the foreigners point toward imperialism from the North, the latter episodes allude to the actual regime, with interrogations, tortures, executions, disappeared, etc.[33]

For a reading that exhausts itself in the work of identifying all the allegorical equivalencies, there is nothing left to say after such a pronouncement; for once it has been established that "the allegory is obvious," all hermeneutical work can be considered over and done. And yet one cannot help but feel that this impoverished notion of allegory as a one-to-one table of equivalencies between a narrative and a politico-historical commentary is inadequate for understanding the deployment of this figure in Donoso's novel. In what follows, I thus outline the novel's critical relationship with the figure of allegory and explore its relevance for understanding the historical conjuncture out of which the novel emerged.

One of the most important insights that Benjamin's study of seventeenth-century Baroque allegory has produced is the idea that allegory is a transitional mode of thinking. It is a figure that rises to prominence in historically specific moments of representational crisis. In the case of the Baroque era, Benjamin posits allegory as a mediating figure between the divine and the secular. When an older mode of representation enters into crisis (the divine) and its successor has not yet established itself (some form of the secular), allegory emerges as a figure that is able to express what cannot, or what can no longer, be stated in conventional ways. Within its narrative structure, allegory grafts together the residual and the emergent (in Benjamin's study this corresponds to the sacred and the profane), enabling it to gesture toward the coming of a new emergent formation. According to Fredric Jameson, allegory is the figure that undertakes this transitional task because unlike the symbol or the metaphor, it is both narrative and discontinuous; its inner dynamic is modeled around a relationship of breaks, gaps, discontinuities, inner distances, and incommensurabilities.[34] In the field of Latin American literary criticism, Idelber Avelar's *The Untimely Present* has explored Benjamin's insights on allegory in order to understand the postdictatorial period. Reading allegory through Benjamin and de Man, Avelar proclaims "the epochal primacy of allegory in postdictatorship tout court" and identifies this primacy of the allegorical with the passage to planetary capitalism.[35] I propose a different reading, one that has less to do with the periods of decline and defeat that mark Benjamin's *Trauerspiel* book (the work of mourning and melancholy) and focuses instead on Benjamin's later work (*The Arcades Project*), which explores the relationship between allegory and commodity culture. From this perspective what needs to be accounted for in the dictatorship and postdictatorship period is the failure of allegory as a transitional mode of thinking. I read *Casa de campo* as a monument to this failure, one caused by allegory being surpassed and made obsolete by commodity abstraction.

One of the ambitions behind Benjamin's decision to study German tragic drama is to put the seventeenth century in relation to the nineteenth century. By doing so, he puts allegorical abstraction into direct relation with the commodity form. The two prove to share some striking similarities. Allegorization and commodification are both processes of debasing the "thingliness" of things. In both cases objects are no longer meaningful in themselves; they can only point to a ghostly meaning that does not inhabit their material realm (in the case of allegory this would be an abstract meaning or commentary, and in the case of commodification it would be exchange value). Thus allegory equates a narrative and its allegorical code the way commodity exchange equates incommensurable use-values. For Benjamin this is made manifest in the work of Charles Baudelaire: "The key to the allegorical form in Baudelaire is bound up with the specific signification which the commodity acquires by virtue of its price. The singular debasement of things through their signification, something characteristic of seventeenth-century allegory, corresponds to the singular debasement of things through their price as commodities."[36] The significance of this inner homology between the allegorical figure and the commodity form can be elucidated by returning to the problem of allegory as a transitional mode of thinking. If allegory comes into prominence during periods of representational crisis and permits a way of gesturing at what is still unsayable about an emergent formation, then the commodity form represents the resolution of this crisis and the effective end of the transition. When Benjamin is looking at nineteenth-century allegory in Baudelaire, it is already an antiquated mechanism, one that has been perfected, intensified, and rendered obsolete by capital's globalizing logic. As Richard Halpern has suggested, the commodity exceeds and surpasses allegory: "The commodity renders allegory obsolete by perfecting and globalizing the latter's logic of representation."[37] The commodity's speculative forms of abstraction are an intensification and an overcoming of allegory. The crucial question is therefore—if Benjamin understands the cultural forms of commodity capitalism through the allegorical fragment, how can we begin to understand the speculative cultural forms of finance capitalism?

Casa de campo is organized around two events: the adult Venturas' excursion away from the country house and their return after the day when everything changed (the revolution). In the period between these two events, time in the house stops, establishing the order of allegory. After violently restoring order to the house, the servants exacerbate this temporal arrest by confiscating all the clocks, calendars, chronometers, and pendulums and by painting all the windows black to make day indistinguishable from night. This is characteristic of allegorical time, where the linear progression of time is petrified, so that past and present do not come together by the movement of a redemptive history (this would be how symbolic time works), but rather through the echoes produced across the abyss of frozen time (this is the notion of a present that is not a transition, but has come to a stop, which is so important for Benjamin). This period during which the young Venturas are abandoned in the country home is marked by a series of conflicting utopian projects. Among these different revolutionary enterprises upon which the cousins embark, the "spears project" is unique. It appears in the novel as the project with the greatest emancipatory potential: it is the most self-reflexive, the most imaginative, and the least likely to simply reproduce yet another orthodoxy. The spears constitute the fence that marks the limit of the Venturas' land and the land of the so-called cannibals. Mauro, one of the older cousins, becomes obsessed with one of the spears and seeks to possess it. He comes to realize that the spear is irreproducible, and it is precisely its unexchangeability, its singular quality, that fascinates him. He proceeds to dig around the base of each spear in order to free them from the regular seriality of the fence. This interruptive work opens for Mauro "a window onto the infinite," and thus is born the emancipatory project of loosening, removing, and returning each spear to its place.

This project is strongly contrasted with the others that the Ventura cousins are developing. It is characterized by lacking any utility at a moment when everyone is throwing themselves into collective action or action that has "implacably defined effects."[38] The spears project is described as a poetic project, an irrelevant game where, according to the narrator, "the liberation was only intellectual, theoretical, but it was enough, or it would be enough when it was completed."[39] The spears project's emancipatory potential lies in its counterallegorical and counterfetishistic moves. It attempts to interrupt the allegorical work of establishing equivalencies among incommensurable things by restituting their materiality. According to Georg Lukács, allegory fetishizes its object in that it "wholly abolishes detail and concrete objective representation" and achieves "a radical annihilation of all particularity."[40] The spears project works against what the novel presents as an enslaving and fetishistic allegory by returning to the spears their status as a determinate particular or, to use Lukács's term, their "unfetishized thinghood." From a Lukacsian perspective this would ally the spears project with the defetishizing tradition of critical realist writing. They both aspire to a true knowledge of things (constructed from their material qualities and details) as mediators of human relations.

In the end the spears project loses its way. The realization that previous generations had already begun the project throws Mauro into a crisis: instead of constituting a single language for his rebellion, the project is trivialized by simply becoming a repetition of what prior generations had done. At this moment the project changes; the action itself becomes its only reason for being. It is no longer about revealing the singularity of each spear and rescuing them from the prison of seriality, but about pure action, and around this everyone is mobilized and starts pulling out spears. It becomes a positive, collective project but, at the same time, a degraded and antiintellectual one. As a result of this co-option, Mauro, initially the most imaginative and poetic of the cousins, ends up becoming the most militant and dogmatic soldier in Adriano Gomara's revolution. This change marks a move from a critical realism to a normative social realism.

Casa de campo takes on the challenge of what kind of writing is possible after the 1973 military coup, the collapse of the national popular project along with its national allegorical narratives, and the neoliberal transformation of Chile. In the episode concerning the spears, we are presented with a double bind. There is on the one hand a critique of what makes allegory so suitable to the experience of the modern—the serial tyranny that its fetishizing and dematerializing logic produces (which can also be understood as a critique of its overlap with the commodity form). But at the same time we are faced with the failure of its alternative—a defetishizing realist discourse capable of returning us to the materiality of things. I want to suggest that this double bind signals a deeper problem, the failure of allegory to function in the Benjaminian sense as a transitional discourse. If nineteenth-century commodity logic has intensified, surpassed, and made obsolete allegorical abstraction, then what role can it play in understanding the epochal crisis and transition that the 1973 military coup represents? The answer to this is not to be found in Donoso; his contribution to the discussion is to signal the crisis and the limits of allegory as a transitional modality. The task of proposing alternatives to or ways out of this crisis has fallen on the shoulders of the writers, thinkers, and artists who have followed him.

2

LITERATURE AND LABOR

Post-Fordism and Human Capital in Diamela Eltit and Arturo Fontaine

Andrés Wood's celebrated 2004 film *Machuca* presents a revisionist reading of the history of Chile's Popular Unity period. It is a reading of history that suggests that the social transformations advanced by the Chilean socialist revolution were annulled in a single instance of violence. In the film's penultimate scene, Gonzalo Infante—the young upper-middle-class protagonist—is threatened by a soldier raiding a shantytown on the eve of the 11 September 1973 military coup. This scene inverts the logic of dedifferentiation that all the preceding parts of *Machuca* develop: focusing on the friendship between two young boys from different socioeconomic backgrounds, the film depicts the dedifferentiation of class spheres that took place during the Popular Unity period, specifically in relation to the school system.[1] And yet during the scene described above—the film's decisive moment—Gonzalo performs an act of radical differentiation: threatened with sharing his friend's fate as all around him the inhabitants of the burning shantytown are being brutalized and killed by soldiers, Gonzalo separates himself from the violence by drawing the soldier's attention to his new Adidas sneakers: "No, no, no! I have nothing to do with it! I'm not from here! I have nothing to do with it! I am from the other side of the river! Look at me!"[2]

The soldier scans Gonzalo from top to bottom, registering the logos that identify his class status, and orders him to leave. Thus branded by the multinational corporations whose interests the military coup served, Gonzalo is insulated from the violence that has been let loose. This moment presents an image of the past with which subsequent Chilean history—even after the trials, corruption scandal, and death of Augusto Pinochet in 2006—is still reckoning. The image of Gonzalo, his Adidas sneakers, and the terror burning all around him makes visible the hidden union between fascistic violence and commodity fetishism that is the ground for the project of neoliberal modernization. This chapter is an exploration of that ground.

The film ends with a fleeing Gonzalo furiously pedaling his red bicycle away from the wreckage that is piling up all around him. Previously the red bicycle appeared as an optimistic allegory of Popular Unity's socialist project of modernity. The two boys from different class backgrounds rode double on the shiny commodity, crossing the distance between the private school and the shantytown. But in the end, fleeing on his bicycle from the wreckage, Gonzalo appears as an Angelus Novus in reverse: his back is toward the catastrophic past (the destruction of Popular Unity and, more generally, the national popular project in Latin America), and his pedaling aligns him with the storm of progress (the dictatorship as a machine of modernity) that pushes him into the future. This storm leads him out of the *población* and to the safety of his mother's new house in an affluent Santiago neighborhood—a product of her affair with the sinister backroom coup plotter expertly played by Federico Luppi—where the spoils of war, the documents of barbarism, are being sorted and hung on a wall by an interior designer.

I begin with this brief reflection on *Machuca* because of the film's double movement: it makes visible the founding union of violence and commodification that lies at the heart of Chilean neoliberal modernization, and it simultaneously closes the possibility of a unique experience of the past (the legacy of the Popular Unity period) by annulling it in a single instance of violence. In what follows I will develop some of the consequences of the first insight by exploring the transformation that the concept of labor undergoes in a thoroughly economized society; in the process I hope to open up the possibility of establishing a unique experience with the past.

Consumption and the Neoliberal Condition

Tomás Moulian's 1997 book, *Chile actual: Anatomía de un mito,* identifies two major economic transformations that mark post-1973 Chile: a vertiginously rapid process of deindustrialization and the massification of credit. This, according to Moulian, "is the doorway to the paradise of consumption that goes through the purgatory of debt."[3] He goes on to document and describe a new regime of "plastic money" and the new subject that emerges from it, "the credit card citizen," which corresponds to a new kind of capitalist state, the neoliberal state. For Moulian this is a thoroughly conservative transformation. It is a form of depoliticization that favors individual strategies instead of associative ones by, for example, ideologically privileging technical solutions to social problems over political ones. Politics is then no longer the space of deliberation or critical interrogation; the rights that the credit card citizen aspires to are limited to consumer rights. Credit, not unionizing or other collective forms of social relations, becomes the instrument of progress. This pseudo-political rationality renders the social economic and links a reduction in state services to the call for personal responsibility and self-care.

The unorthodox kernel that emerges in Moulian's diagnosis of Chilean consumer society is his attempt to distance himself from a critical tradition—spanning from Fromm to Horkheimer and Adorno and beyond—that has condemned consumerism as the banal product of a mass society and as straightforward alienation. Moulian seeks to combine a model of consumerism as domination with one that connects it to pleasure and excess. As he puts it, using an ecclesiastic homily: "It is the purgatory of a growing exploitation, together with the heaven of amplified consumptive possibilities."[4] At this point Moulian establishes a parallel between his thinking and the work of another scholar of consumption, Néstor García Canclini.

Despite the explicit connection that Moulian makes in his book, there are fundamental differences between the two projects. Canclini would undoubtedly condemn Moulian's pessimistic diagnosis of consumption as yet another repetition of a now familiar dead end: neoliberalism has reduced civil society to an atomized ensemble of anesthetized consumers. Canclini's project, outlined in *Consumers and Citizens,* consists in saving consumption from the naysayers in order—pace thinkers such as Arjun Appadurai and James Holston—to explore its potential as a "site that is good for thinking," that is, a privileged space to witness the emergence of new forms of social organization.[5] By stressing how commodities are actively selected, used, and appropriated, Canclini folds consumption in on itself to reveal the emancipatory seeds for the reconstitution of public spaces.

Canclini laments the anachronistic nineteenth-century approach to culture that the Latin American state cultural bureaucracies deploy; their almost exclusive support of literature, painting, and music to the detriment of more popular and audiovisual genres such as modern urban rock and hip-hop, comics, soap operas, and videos. The error, according to Canclini, is that in our contemporary world the aesthetic foundations of citizenship are to be found in the latter, not in the former. For it is in these media spaces that the desire for community and social cohesion is supposedly being manifested. These new communities are no longer territorially, linguistically, or politically bound, but rather are groups that cluster around symbolic consumption (soccer matches, raves, chat rooms, Facebook, Twitter, etc.). Thus deterritorialized, "culture becomes a process of multi-national assemblage, a flexible articulation of parts, a montage of features that any citizen in any country, of whatever religion or ideology can read and use."[6] Although Canclini acknowledges some of the tensions and contradictions that are part of the subsumption of the older collective relations to these new individualistic organizations, he concludes that the greater good is in the expansion of these associations of consumers.

If Moulian's critique of consumer society slips by mistakenly allying itself with Canclini's project, then Canclini's attempt to think emancipation through consumption slips by employing Diamela Eltit's *El padre mío* as an example. *Citizens and Consumers* concludes by citing the following *El padre mío* passage as an "apt description of this drama of dispersed social communication": "Newspaper scraps, fragments of extermination, syllables of death, fake pauses, commercial phrases, the names of the dead. It is a deep crisis of language, an infection of memory, a disarticulation of all ideologies. It is a shame, I thought. It is Chile, I thought."[7] For a book that purports to emancipate itself from a poetics of disenchantment, this is a very strange connection to make. For the shame that Eltit refers to is not a "flexible accumulation" or a "multi-national assemblage" of newsprint, extermination, death, lies, slogans, and names of the dead that any consumer/citizen can, toolbox style, use, select, or appropriate as they see fit. The crisis in language, the infection of memory, the disarticulation of all ideologies signals a deeper catastrophe, a crisis of representation. In response to this crisis, the *testimonio El padre mío* answers in a schizophrenic discourse that strips language to its most literal, most cryptic realism. It is the text that most radically exemplifies the discourse of melancholy: not only is it contrary or dissident, but it undermines the very grammar of signification and the means of representation. In this sense, the Eltit citation is a ghostly incrustation that brings to the surface something that has been repressed throughout Canclini's book, that is, the interruptive work of the incommensurable, the untranslatable, the unexchangeable singularity of loss. Canclini wants to go beyond hermeneutics—more specifically a hermeneutics he considers entrenched in the work of the negative—in order to develop a research agenda capable of constructing "a rationality that can encompass everyone's reasoning as well as the structure of conflicts and negotiations."[8] Eschewing frameworks that he deems "irrational," Canclini strives to assess consumption on the basis of rational ideological principles. This is, of course, precisely what the marginal subject of the *testimonio* Canclini cites refuses to do.

I take Moulian's gesture toward a new thinking about consumption as indicative of the transformation in the logic of capital that he himself diagnoses. The need to inquire into and account for the pleasurable, the excessive, and the wasteful aspects of consumption breaks with a productivist and utilitarian tradition of political economy. It suggests that the old bourgeois values of sobriety and asceticism are less relevant for understanding contemporary capitalism than qualities such as creative risk taking, gambling, novelty, and difference. Within this scheme, Canclini's notion of a deterritorialized consumer community (territorially, linguistically, and politically unbound) parallels finance capital's logic of abstraction. It decodes older identity-coding systems and liberates them for new and more functional combinations. *El padre mío*'s presence in Canclini's text highlights the tensions and contradictions that erupt as the transition attempts to incorporate residual figures not yet effectively subsumed by this speculative logic.

The following two sections of this essay explore analogous literary interruptions of the transition described above with a focus on the models of labor (human capital and post-Fordism) that emerge in the context of the consumerist transformations Moulian and Canclini describe.

Arturo Fontaine's *Oír su voz* and the Logic of Human Capital

In a 2002 interview the Chilean writer and critic Armando Uribe recalled the following anecdote about Arturo Fontaine's first novel:

> At that moment [Fontaine] was writing *Oír su voz,* and he told me what the novel was about. I found it very interesting because it contained a great deal that was of a financial, economic, and political nature. When he finished it he turned it in to his workshop director who at the time was Donoso. And Donoso told him how was it possible that he included things like financial institutions and everything related to the economic bust of the 1980s, which no one understood or was interested in, even though it had been a very important collective chilean experience. Donoso also told him that he should include adultery because that did interest people, and this turned out to be the weakest part of the novel. That reveals a case of disconnection from reality.[9]

Uribe identifies two relevant points for the discussion that will follow: the significance that the novel's incorporation of the discourse of economics represents and the complex relation that Fontaine and other writers of his generation have with José Donoso. In regard to the latter, any notion of a simple or direct continuity between these writers needs to be abandoned, as does the ideologically charged recourse to "influence." I contend that *Oír su voz* is indebted to Donoso's narrative project, specifically to the transition that his works enact from a "gold standard" of representation associated with the realist novel to one based on "fictitious capital" (chapter 1). For this reason *Oír su voz,* many of whose chapters read like a treatise on political economy, is, as Uribe points out, uncannily unrecognizable as a novel for Donoso. The effect of this, Donoso's supposed "disconnection from reality," remits to a sea change, a transition where the cultural expressions of older forms begin to become as incomprehensible to the present as the present forms have become to the past.

Arturo Fontaine's 1992 novel *Oír su voz* fills pages and pages with the specialized language of monetarism (stocks, bonds, value-added tax, interest rates, internal return rate, land speculation, debt, and credit). The reader is immersed in the world of private companies, the stock exchange, Banco de Chile functionaries, and a group of entrepreneurs centered around the Banco Agrícola e Industrial (a small bank nationalized during the Popular Unity period and then privatized during the dictatorship). The narrative is also intercalated with advertising clips, television executives' pitches for advertising campaigns, and the descriptive labels of commodity items such as suntanning lotion. This saturation of the novel with the discourse of political economics, where even the characters function as abstract economic conceptualizations, corresponds to a general economization of life during the boom-and-bust years of the late 1970s and early 1980s in Chile.[10] The central conflict that the novel attempts to resolve can be framed as the neutralization of the tensions and contradictions that emerge as new notions of abstraction, labor, and social relations, which are modeled on the stock market, human capital, and depoliticized consumerism (represented by the Aliro Toro financial group), subsume older traditional forms (represented by the figure of Pelayo Fernández, the displaced and melancholic *latifundista* heir who is haunted by his agrarian past).

The author of *Oír su voz,* Arturo Fontaine Talavera, is the director of the Centro de Estudios Públicos, a center-right-wing think tank dedicated to the circulation of liberal and neoliberal thinkers such as Frederich von Hayek, Karl Popper, Ludwig von Mises, and Milton Friedman, among others; public policy discussions; and the coordination and circulation of public opinion polls.[11] A self-defined right-wing thinker, Fontaine has been a champion of the Chilean "economic miracle," referring to it as a "new paradigm in Latin America."[12] In his essay writing, he has expressed his belief in the benefits of the social economy of the market; his essay "Reflexiones sobre ética y mercado" makes the claim—during the height of the dictatorship—that there is an essential equivalency between intellectual liberty (the conditions for creativity and originality) and market liberty (free trade, deregulation, competition, open economies). Elsewhere he has argued that Chile bridges two fundamental elements of contemporary globalization: religion and economics.[13] He sees in the figure of the Chilean businessman both the modern and cosmopolitan elements associated with socioeconomic globalization and the family-values-oriented, ethical-religious conservatism associated with religious globalization. The first of these two arguments is a classic example of the logic of neoliberal dedifferentiation, where the values associated with intellectual liberty are subsumed into the logics of an economic order. The second attempts the ideological operation of trying to seamlessly bring together two disparate discourses under the common banner of a project of modernity (sans secularization).

Commercially *Oír su voz* was a relatively successful novel, although it received mixed literary reviews. The most scathing of these came from Ignacio Valente, the influential Opus Dei critic who wrote for *El Mercurio*. In his review Valente describes *Oír su voz* as dull, slow, tedious, common, "chata" (flat and shallow), full of stereotypes, badly written, lacking inner density, and creating inauthentic worlds, and dismisses the novel as an accumulation of data with little literary merit.[14] On the question of literary merit I share little common ground with Valente, yet I do tend to agree with many of his judgments of this particular novel. These aesthetic shortcomings notwithstanding, *Oír su voz*'s value is that, in spite of itself, it makes visible the forces of transformation in a specific moment in Chilean history. How then do we approach Fontaine's literary work? Is it simply an aesthetic extension of his neoliberal project? This kind of deterministic reading is an a priori dead end, incapable of producing light or real insight, stuck in the reproduction—and easy condemnation—of what we already know. I read the description of Chilean society that Fontaine elaborates in *Oír su voz* from the standpoint of the literary tradition in which the novelist situates himself: Balzaquian realism. The idea here is that the realist form ultimately goes beyond the author's own class sympathies and throws askew the attempts at ideological closure. Neil Larsen's reading of Mario Vargas Llosa's "The Realist as Neoliberal" is a good example of this strategy. What Larsen says of Vargas Llosa can also be said of Fontaine: the realist storyteller ultimately eludes the neoliberal ideologue.[15]

In the tradition of Balzac's symbolic narratives of class representatives, Fontaine's novel gives a taxonomical account of a new emerging entrepreneurial class. The foil to the new breed of neoliberal entrepreneur—represented in the novel by the "Chicago boys" Mempo Tamburini and Aliro Toro—is Rubén Eskanazi.[16] He represents "the old school Latin American business man." [17] From the perspective of the "Chicago boys," Eskanazi embodies all that is wrong about the old business world. He is "without principles, unscrupulously opportunistic, with a family fortune built from oligopolistic governmental exemptions and maintained through cunning, avarice, utility withdrawals used to make international deposits, and a lack of imagination."[18] A vestige of a residual capitalist era, Eskanazi is never in debt because he never risks anything. He has no projects in his head that he is passionate about or any new ideas on how to produce wealth. This contrast between the old-school businessmen and the young piranhas marks one of the fundamental transformations in the logic of capital that Fontaine's novel explores: conventional bourgeois values (sobriety, thrift, work ethic, calculation, and foresight) no longer correspond to the demands of contemporary capitalism. The kind of petty calculation and expected profit return that structured the world of a character like Rubén Eskanazi is of little use to the likes of Mempo Tamburini or Aliro Toro (the young piranhas based on the "Chicago boy" economists), who need to imagine and create a demand before there even is one. The work of the new entrepreneurs is premised on the characteristics of creative artistic activity, rather than the cold calculating reason associated with previous eras of capitalist accumulation. In this new economy the old stalwarts of thrift, sobriety, and asceticism give way to risk, unpredictability, undecidability, and virtuosity: "A business does not require capital, or anything. Everything can be bought or rented. That is what the market is for. What is of value is the concept. And the concept is always an anticipation. . . . That is why we live hanging from the future that we invented. Our current riches sprout from that which still does not exist, from tomorrow, I mean, from what it will cost tomorrow."[19] Here a premium is put on creation, anticipating trends, identifying and interpreting indicators, on performing in a highly subjective and often arbitrary medium. It is all about gambling on novelty, surprise, and difference.

In the novel the groundwork for this new economical thinking is laid by the transitional figure Antonio Barraza. A character that is always in the background, Barraza creates the necessary conditions for the new generation of Chilean entrepreneurs. He is the vice-president of the Banco de Estado and ligates the work of the state and the work of the market, appeasing the inconsistencies between authoritarian rule and free-market reforms and bridging the incommensurable gap between economic development and human suffering.

Across the street from his undistinguished office in the Banco de Estado—from which extends "state power over the value of the most commerciable good of all, money"—is the government building La Moneda, whose name derives from being the place where money was fabricated. Thus we get "La Moneda's two faces of power: the monopoly over violence and the fabrication of money."[20] With these two faces, Barraza embodies the seemingly incongruous wedlock that marked the Chilean transition: strong state authoritarian rule and unprecedented neoliberal economic reforms.

Barraza begins his career with an academic interest in economics. He is a pre–Chicago School economist known for his heterodox economic theories. He studied at the Massachusetts Institute of Technology and Cambridge, working with thinkers such as John Maynard Keynes, Joan V. Robinson, Oskar R. Lange, and Ronald L. Meek, mixing them into a "post-Keynesian" discourse.[21] The failure of his intellectual project (to write a groundbreaking book on economics) produces a radical conversion in Barraza.

Following a now-familiar path from the intellectual work of producing a book to the biopolitical art of government, Barraza "converted himself into the inspiring and concealed surgeon of a vast and complex operation of social engineering."[22] This biopolitical transformation is what Michel Foucault evokes with his often-cited statement that at the threshold of the modern age, life is what is at stake in politics.[23] Barraza's biopolitical project imagines a transformation with the ambition, depth, and magnitude of England's Industrial Revolution, Ludwig Erhardt's West German social-market miracle, and the Korean economic leap under General Park.

The basic tools for this project of social engineering are the neoliberal reforms Barraza initiates. Under Barraza's social-engineering revolution, economic analytical schemata and the criteria for economic decision making are applied to spheres that are not exclusively economic. Economism becomes the official language, and Barraza's greatest triumph is "implementing this new official language, which is equivalant to Sanskrit in ancient India or French in nineteenth-century St. Petersburg."[24] This marks an important shift from trying to govern society in the name of the economy (a classical liberal free-market strategy) to redefining the social sphere as an economic domain (neoliberalism proper). The economy is no longer considered one social domain among others, but an area that embraces the entirety of human action. Thus, rational economic action becomes the all-encompassing principle of legitimation. An extreme example of this is Barraza's calculation of that which lies beyond measure: the fate of the tortured and disappeared versus the advantages of economic development: "And he had the scientific certainty of knowing the cure: it was an injectable preparation. Lamentable, but effective. The military allowed him to put it in place. The calculation of that pain did not frighten him."[25] Barraza's shadowy presence is a constant reminder of the authoritarian violence on which the new economists' temple of speculation is built.

If Eskanazi represents a vestigial figure of capitalism's oligarchic days and Barraza is the biopolitical mastermind behind the neoliberal transition, then Mempo Tamburini and Aliro Toro are the prototype "Chicago boys." They represent an emerging entrepreneurial class that displaces politicians and intellectuals. They are technocrats with PhDs applying rational-choice science to the whole social field. Of the two, Aliro Toro is most dynamic and aggressive of the new entrepreneurs depicted in the novel. In Toro's case the agrarian reform is not a traumatic event that displaces him from a traditional world, but an opportunity he seizes upon to build an economic empire. To accomplish this he capitalizes on the opening up of land speculation and the agricultural boom. Toro embodies the defining characteristics of the emerging financial elite—he is described in the novel as both a new kind of conquistador and an *encomendero.* Perhaps the most central of these characteristics is the category of abstraction as it is configured by finance capital. Although his fortunes were built on the agricultural boom, Aliro Toro never visits his vineyards or *granja marinas:* "He preferred to maintain his distance and not get caught up in the corporeity of those productive processes that, in the mind of the financier, are only another kind of promissory note. He liked it that the object of his passion took abstract forms." [26] The notion of abstraction that begins to emerge here refers to an emptying of stable substances and their unifying identifications (the different kinds of crops and their value in gold or silver); an immateriality of the commodity (its value is no longer found in itself, in its weight or measure, but like money, it is always outside itself); and the quality of endless transferability. From the cycle of revolutions—the agrarian reform being one of the most important—that led to the collapse of the old oligarchic order emerges a new capitalist regime that recodifies, under the banner of abstraction, older forms of commodities and commodity relations. In the example above, Toro's agricultural world is stripped of all the traditional relations once associated with it and emptied of its content. It is transformed into "a green and luxurious denseness like a jungle. A 'gold mine,' he thought, 'of vegetable gold.'" [27] In this sense Toro is the most radical of the characters in the novel; he has no attachments to the previous social world and fully embraces the market values of the emergent one.

The novel's "Chicago boys" have a monetarist focus: "Because money," deliberates Mempo, "had the virtue of transmuting the life of a person and giving them that mysterious and irresistable halo, that recognition, that image of success and solidity that nothing and no one can deny." [28] The idea advanced is that all values are relative (happiness, fame, triumph, power, honor) but "money is always . . . money. When all else fails, when things go down, only Sir Money continues to be Sir Money." [29] The irony that the novel is very aware of is that money itself has no value; it can only remit to a value that lies outside of itself. This monetary emphasis corresponds to what has been described as the vulgar economist's move from labor to money as the source of value, resulting in a situation where "money begets money." Mempo's fall into economic and social ruin at the novel's end is, the reader is led to believe, tied to his rationalist limitations. Although fascinated by the flash and speed of this turbulent new world of high finance, he is unable to let go of his bourgeois inhibitions in order to fully embrace the all-or-nothing risks of finance capitalism. He remains, to the very end, tethered to the illusion of calculability and predictability instilled in him by his economic training. This is, ultimately, the deciding difference between Mempo Tamburini and Aliro Toro: the latter is the economic wonder child who emerges unscathed from each market crisis and economic scandal, always foreseeing his investment in the next empire-building venture.

Oír su voz is a novel about the economization of life where the always intensifying process of reification attempts to resolve the tensions and contradictions that surface as neoliberal capitalist accumulation subsumes previous forms of capitalist accumulation. What emerges in the novel's representation of this process—specifically in the entrepreneurial figures I have described above—is a shift in the way labor is conceptualized. *Oír su voz* can be read as a literary treatise on the concept of human capital and on the conceptualization of the worker as an entrepreneur of himself.

Human capital refers to the different sets of skills and talents that a subject can acquire by investing in education, training, hobbies, and any other activity that could potentially increase his or her value in the workplace. The science of human capital seeks to quantify the value of that investment. Michel Foucault's work on biopolitics and neoliberalism provides some insights into the logic of human capital. For Foucault the defining characteristic of American-style neoliberalism is the dual process of extending economic analyses into previously unexplored domains and the application of an economic model to a sphere of human action previously thought to be noneconomic. Taking this premise as his starting point, Foucault focuses his study of neoliberal biopolitics on its concept of labor, human capital.[30] Human capital breaks with the temporal determinism that characterizes much of classical political economy's reflections on labor.[31] It shifts the focus from production, exchange, and consumption to "substitutable choices"; its emphasis is not on material goods but on the science of human behavior.[32] Labor is conceptualized as something that cannot be abstracted from an individual worker; instead of being a commodity, it is an inherent skill, an ability, a technology of the self. For Foucault this signals a transformation in the study of economics: it marks the move from the analysis of the historical logic of processes (classical economics) to "the analysis of the internal rationality, the strategic programming of individuals' activity," or, in a word, biopolitics.[33] There is a return to *Homo economicus,* not in the classical sense of a partner of exchange, but rather as an entrepreneur of himself: the worker is conceived as his own capital, his own producer, his own source of earnings.[34]

If *Oír su voz* serves as a literary treatise on human capital, then its equivalent in the sphere of Chilean economic discourse is a document written in 1973 known as *El ladrillo: Bases de la política económica del Gobierno Militar Chileno*. The text provides a blueprint for turning back the tide on more than forty years of import-substitution industrialization and for a return to the liberal period that predates the 1930s Great Depression. The story goes that on 11 September 1973 the photocopying machines at Editorial Lord Cochrane worked nonstop to duplicate copies of the lengthy document and that by midday on Wednesday, 12 September, the general officers of the armed forces all had copies of the plan on their desks.[35] The history of the document dates back to 1969, when a team of economists—loosely affiliated with the Universidad Católica and many of whose members had participated in the exchange program with the University of Chicago—comes together to develop a socioeconomic plan for the right-wing presidential candidate Jorge Alessandri. Alessandri's electoral defeat by Salvador Allende temporarily disbands the team, but they reunite in 1973 to map a way out of the crisis that the authors associate with Popular Unity's socialist project. The end product is a 193-page antistatist text whose utopian project is the creation of a world free of centralized planning and bureaucratic direction, where consumers are free to access the market's multinational assemblage of features.

El ladrillo is, in and of itself, an unremarkable economic text—for the most part, it limits itself to mechanical application of the work of Milton Friedman, Gary Becker, and other Chicago School professors to the Chilean context—but it does reveal fundamental elements of the Chilean neoliberal project. As Gabriel Valdés has suggested, the experience of reading the document conjures up the effects that the Brazilian cultural critic Roberto Schwarz calls "out of place ideas." *El ladrillo*'s attempt to suture so-called liberatory ideals onto an authoritarian regime produces an "ideology to the second degree," where ultimately reality is not being described, not even falsely.[36] How else can one understand statements made by Sergio De Castro, one of *El ladrillo*'s authors, such as, "A person's actual freedom can only be ensured through an authoritarian regime"?[37]

El ladrillo repeatedly stresses that all of its assessments and proposals are based on "eminently technical criteria." This appeal to a strictly technical knowledge appears in the text as an alternative to the ideologically charged period that marks its conception; for it is ideological thinking, the text stresses, that created the chaos that ultimately led to the military coup. Taken even further, the turn to a knowledge based on "purely technical criteria" is a turn to a postpolitical politics based on the logic of market pragmatism, cost-benefit analysis, and the figure of *Homo economicus.* It augurs the transition from the reign of the politician, the revolutionary, and the intellectual to the reign of the expert, the technician, and the technocrat.

The other notable characteristic of *El ladrillo* is its emphasis on establishing a new model of labor. The text attempts to reorganize Chilean labor utilizing the concept of human capital. Through a capital investment in education, culture, social integration, health, and diet, the human-capital labor model is proposed as the new path for Chilean modernization.[38] One of the intentional consequences of replacing the labor model associated with import-substitution industrialization with the model of human capital is the undermining of one of the traditional strengths of the Chilean left, the working class. The worker is replaced with an entrepreneur of himself or, in Tomás Moulian's term, the credit-card citizen invested in individual strategies of personal responsibility and self-care.

Both *El ladrillo* and *Oír su voz* serve as primers for understanding the increasingly dominant logic of human capital in Chile. *El ladrillo* deploys the concept in a prescriptive register—as a blueprint for reengineering Chilean modernity after the Popular Unity period. *Oír su voz* narrativizes human capital's emergence in a story about a transition: the subsumption of a traditional mostly agrarian and *latifundista* society by a regime of accumulation characterized by the logic of neoliberal capitalism. Fontaine's novel not only formally incorporates the language of monetarism and explicitly references the economization of life under neoliberal capitalism; it indexes the emerging logic of human capital in Chilean society. Beginning with the biopolitical groundwork set by Barraza, which attempts to ideologically suture together the impossible contradictions between authoritarian rule and free-market reforms, the novel explores the emergence of a new breed of entrepreneurs who break with the financial old guard. These "entrepreneurs of themselves" are purveyors of human capital: value is delinked from income or from accumulated potential and associated with strategies of self-appreciation. In the world depicted in these two texts, all human behavior, actions, and decisions become part of a portfolio-valorizing project.

Diamela Eltit: From the Art of the Refractory to *Mano de obra*

The work of Diamela Eltit, both as a member of the visual arts collective Colectivo de Acciones de Arte (CADA) and as a writer, became for a specific period of Chilean history synonymous with the most critical elements of the postdictatorship scene. The disparate discourses that dwell under the rubric of postdictatorship converged, at least momentarily, in that they expressed fundamental differences with the state (both dictatorial and transitional) and some of the dominant elements of the social sciences.[39] Faced with an official discourse espousing political consensus and reconciliation, and attempting to smooth over the contradictions of a pacted transition to democracy fraught with impunity and simulated justice, postdictatorship discourse distinguishes itself as an acutely critical space. It eschewed the epic work of weaving recuperative narratives connecting the present to a long democratic tradition (this would imply adopting a limited notion of the military coup as merely a parenthesis within a larger democratic project). In the broadest terms, it explored and pushed the limits of the crisis initiated by the coup in terms of the possibilities and impossibilities of thinking politics, history, and representation.

Nelly Richard has stated that the postdictatorship scene dwells under the aegis of melancholy: "Trauma, mourning and melancholy

. . . are figures that . . . lent their affective tone to the expression of postdictatorship, an expression marked by the problematic character of a tension between *loss of knowledge* (of confidence in knowledge as a secure foundation) and *knowledge of loss* (the critical vindication of waste, of the *remainder,* as the condition of a thought of an afterwards now irreconcilable with previous models of finitude and the totalization of truth)."[40] Postdictatorship's emphasis on the fragmentary, the refractory, the residual, and the allegorical works within the logic of the purported ethical primacy that melancholy has over mourning. This ethical primacy has to do with the impossibility of introjecting (the process of substitution and exchange that defines the work of mourning) the melancholic remainder and remaining faithful to its unexchangeable singularity. Thus, against the subsumption of differential subjectivities in the assimilative logic of the market, the melancholic response is the always "unresolved remainder," the "unassimilable residue," the unexchangeable singularity of loss. It is in these figures that postdictatorship invests its critical potential.

The critical work of a text like Eltit's *testimonio El padre mío,* whose interruptive effects I describe in regards to Canclini's project at the beginning of this essay, make it an exemplary articulation of the challenges and problems of melancholy. For if melancholy, understood as the unexchangeable singularity of loss, mistrusts any form of representation (its often-quoted rejection of metaphor being only the most obvious example), then how does the melancholic text refer to the object whose loss it laments? *El padre mío* answers this in a cryptic, unparseable, paradoxical, and reiterative register; a schizophrenic discourse that strips language to its most literal, most cryptic realism. It is perhaps best understood as a refractory text. *Refractory,* as in a complete negation and as a change in course, refers to cultural practices that are inspired by Benjamin's famous preface: "The concepts which are introduced into the theory of art in what follows differ from the more familiar terms in that they are completely useless for the purposes of Fascism."[41] In the case of *El padre mío*'s appropriation of refractory strategies, not only must they be useless for the purposes of fascism, but they must also elude the political orthodoxy of the militant left that attempts to reintegrate all the broken symbols into a new totality ("make whole what has been smashed"), the technical reductionism of the executive discourse of the social sciences, and the ubiquitous language of the mass media that axiomatizes all difference. The idea here is not only that refractory strategies are contrary or dissident, but that they work at undermining the very grammar of signification and means of representation that the dominant order employs. A particular reading of Benjamin's work comes into play as a way of thinking about the history of the oppressed as a discontinuity (antihistoricist): loose unconnected fragments, leftovers, a narrative of the residual. This refractory strategy that invests in the fragment the quality of resistance to any incorporating machine (authoritarian, revolutionary, or neoliberal) parallels the melancholic's identification with the lost object and the melancholic remainder's unexchangeable singularity.

This kind of critique is what melancholy does so well; its radical suspicion of all narratives and its intrinsic mistrust of representation confer upon it a privileged form of critique. Yet it is inadequate to take up the other challenge that *El padre mío* poses: what kind of writing is possible at this limit? How can we begin to think about how the relation between the aesthetic and the economic is being rearticulated in neoliberal times? How can we begin to understand the speculative cultural forms of finance capitalism? I maintain that Eltit's novel *Mano de obra* marks a turn away from a refractory poetics to a more direct literary engagement with the problems of commodity fetishism, collective relations, and value in the neoliberal condition. The novel explores the sensuous relation with things, the ambiguous resistance of things, the inevitable disillusion at their failure, and the desire for a fuller access to them. In a sense, the novel marks the beginning of a movement out from the aegis of melancholy.

The first half of *Mano de obra,* which counterpoints the title of each chapter with the material that constitutes it, frames the basic conflict that the novel engages. The titles are named after famous early twentieth-century communist, anarchist, and union newspapers. Eltit invokes the workerist tradition of Chile's past in order to explore work and labor relations under neoliberalism, understood here in Pierre Bourdieu's sense of the systematic destruction of collectives. An important feature of these chapter headings is that each newspaper, which stands in as an expression of collective organization, is concretely fixed to a time and a place (Iquique, 1911; Santiago, 1918; Antofagasta, 1909; Tocopilla, 1904). They are territorialized; in each case the collective cultural expression is tied to a specific place of industrial production (factories, mines, nitrate towns). In opposition, the content of the chapters examines worker and commodity relations in a context where capital takes flight, abandons production, and seeks maximization in nonproductive spaces (the service sector and the supermarket being the most important of these).

The rift that this juxtaposition of heading and chapter produces can be framed in terms of the antagonism between an old form of political representation, *el pueblo,* and the emerging forms under neoliberalism (what Moulian calls the disassociative strategies of the credit-card citizen). If the *pueblo* corresponds to the thinking of the one-one will—one action, one sovereign, one state—then the emerging forms are radically antistate, antipopular, with no political unity or juridical personage. They manifest themselves, as Paolo Virno paraphrasing Hobbes puts it, as "the *Multitude* against the *People*."[42]

In *Mano de obra* these emerging neoliberal forms are explored in that bastion of consumerist activity, the supermarket. The novel examines in all its complexity the relations among supermarket workers, clients, and supervisors and how merchandise mediates them all. Within this optic, against the concept of the *pueblo* emerges a workforce marked by tameness (*mansedumbre*) and conditioned to develop "an extensive labor subservience."[43] With their neutral presence (clean, odorless, expressionless, and pale) the service workers form a material part of the supermarket to such a degree that their whole existence is tied to the order of the supermarket products. When displays are disordered and products ruined, "my existence sinks."[44] When children rip open packaging and handle the products, "in those moments, when a climax of shoddy goods has been unleashed, my life lacks all meaning."[45] The fragility of these subjects is such that any criticism of their work puts their whole existence into question: "The terrible, destructive word that they direct toward me, echoes in my head and makes me feel bad. The word wounds and perforates me, opening a hole in my kidneys. It wounds me. It perforates me. It makes me think that work, to which I dedicate all of my energy, is not worth it."[46] Passivity is fomented to the point that even the thought,

"It is possible that I do not deserve to be treated so badly by the clients," becomes unthinkable.[47] The vociferous demands of yesterday's organized and militant workforce are neutralized: "I bite my tongue. I control it, I punish it to the limit of injury. I bite the pain. And I order my eye."[48] Perhaps the most disturbing example of this is the case of the character Alberto, who, suspected of trying to rally support for a unionizing movement in the supermarket, is treated as a pariah by his coworkers and promptly betrayed to the supervisors by his lover.

A possible transgressive moment is the narrator's encounter with a thief posing as a client. The thief engages in a ritual of seduction in order to establish a degree of intimacy with the narrator and convince her to collude in his project of stealing the products. He is motivated by a desire to simultaneously enjoy the product without paying for it and incriminate her for the crime.[49] In *Mano de obra* even theft is emptied of any contestatory or rebellious potential. It becomes another fetishized form of consumption, another way to "enjoy the merchandise."[50] Instead of putting disconnected groups into relation, it reinforces the contempt and distance between the two subjects as each attempts to betray the other. The narrator, after playing along with the thief, eventually turns him in.[51]

These novelistic descriptions of neoliberal labor relations correspond to, and at times parody, so-called post-Fordist work. Paolo Virno's theorization of post-Fordist work defines it as communicative, affective, and including those abilities that were previously practiced in one's spare time.[52] He begins from the premise that the traditional frontiers separating intellect, work, and action have collapsed. One of the results is that work is no longer condemned to being the sphere of repetitive and predictable automatism; it absorbs the qualities of political action (unforeseeablility, the ability to begin something new, linguistic performances, and the ability to range among alternative possibilities). Within Virno's scheme, service work plays a central role. It was one of two kinds of immaterial labor that Marx condemned as wage labor that is not productive (to obtain a service, one spends income, not capital, he argued), and is thus insignificant for capitalist production. For Virno, service work's mercurial and ambiguous status is the reason that it was never fully understood by political economy, and it becomes, for him, the paradigmatic example of a post-Fordist model of work. It is both a nonproductive form of labor (an activity without a finished product) and imbued with the performance qualities of political action. By displacing production, service work focuses on "modulating social cooperation": that is, the art of the possible, dealing with the unforeseen and profiting from fortuitous opportunities. The poverty of all this—and it is a poverty of which Virno is acutely aware—is that qualities from the sphere of action, like the act of entering into relation with the other and even the possession and valorization of language, are reduced to a function of wage labor.

The supermarket service workers in Eltit's novel, specifically in its second part, are modeled after this post-Fordist notion of "servile virtuosity." Their daily performances are creative responses to a workplace that is constantly revolutionizing itself. The supervisors hire and fire employees at an accelerating rate, always increasing the number of new workers, reducing the hours of work assigned, and driving down wages. The novel focuses on the travails of a group of senior workers as they develop strategies and abilities that will keep them off the supervisor's layoff list. This has little to do with the classic immaterial labor notion of "service with a smile," based rather on the establishment of complex networks of information gathering, the ever-shifting formation of alliances, and the occasional betrayal or sacrifice of a fellow worker. The relations among the supermarket workers also work following the logic of the cyclic accumulation and disposal of things. No ties are ever established among the employees because their coexistence is always temporary; what forcibly brings this community of workers together are the increasingly lowered wages, the reduced hours, and the poor working conditions. Thus, the pact among the workers is forged out of a sense not of solidarity but of survival: "we are obligated to care for each other."[53] The threat of being arbitrarily fired, the cameras, the supervisors, the mutual surveillance between workers, and the self-surveillance enacted by each particular worker imply that the workplace exerts a control on the totality of the workers' lives (eating, shitting, resting, and thinking).

Throughout the novel the visual field appears as the dominant one in a world obsessed with the exterior appearance of things. Yet this fascination with the physical properties of things encompasses all the senses, as demonstrated by the client who has to inspect everything in the store: "he examines the precision of the scales, he checks the solvency and security of the shelves, he squeezes the fruit, smells the meat, calculates the validity and thickness of the milk. Yes, yes, yes, that is what he is doing. He comes to the supermarket to smell, breath, auscultate, handle, beat, kneel down, hide, intercept, try to enter the cellars or spy my name on my apron."[54] What we have here is a heightened interest in the physical properties of objects that has traditionally been linked to literary realism as the cultural form associated with the emergence of a bourgeois class culture. From this perspective, the emergence of realist perceptions and social relations parallels the emergence of exchange value and the equivalence of the money form, which led to a heightened interest in the physical property of objects and intersubjective relations.[55] In other words, the lively human relations developed in nineteenth-century trade and commerce drove merchants and consumers to take a greater interest in the sensory nature of their wares and the psychological traits of their interlocutors. *Mano de obra* obsessively reproduces this realist trait. The consumers are constantly smelling, touching, squeezing, and observing the products. This renewed interest in the physical properties of things doesn't have the secularizing push that is usually associated with the nineteenth-century realist tradition; rather, it creates "a contaminated mysticism": "They touch the products as if they were brushing up against God. They stroke them with a fanatical devotion (which is religiously precipitated)."[56] Besides being a celebration of the physical qualities of things, the supermarket serves as a meeting place. In this sense it also corresponds to the realist focus on the social relations and psychological traits of its subjects. The supermarket is for the present what the factory, the public square, and the bar were for the previous world evoked in the chapter headings: a place to enter into relation with the other. The difference is that far from being a breeding ground for collective social relations, the supermarket is marked by the camera's omniscient surveillance and hateful piercing gaze, which transform the clients and workers into enemies. It is also a place that separates segments of society from the world of products. These are segments, like the elderly, that have become insignificant consumers. The exclusion works in terms of the dominance of the physicality of things; as the old bodies begin to break down, they become an impediment to consumption: they are too slow, they block the aisle, and they disorder the displays. The world of the products becomes unintelligible to them as their eyes can no longer read the miniscule lettering. Expulsed from the world of consumption, they wander the supermarket, killing time until they die.

I read *Mano de obra* as a literary treatise on the emerging logics of labor in a country undergoing radical deindustrialization. The most obvious example of this is the juxtaposition of headers from a previous, territorialized moment of industrial production and their subsumption into the nonplace of the supermarket. The novel explores the new forms of labor and labor relations that emerge in this deterritorialized space. Eltit starts from premises that are similar to the post-Fordist notion of virtuoso work but takes a radically different turn. Eschewing any idealized characterization of the new labor regime as work-cum-action, a dystopic vision emerges that reveals a new regime of domination where the workplace is extended to the point that it encompasses the totality of life.

Coming from radically different ideological points of departure—*Oír su voz* is firmly entrenched in the neoliberal labor logic of human capital, whereas *Mano de obra*'s vision of the supermarket service worker is in dialogue with the post-Fordist concept of immaterial labor—both novels reveal strikingly similar logics. They both signal a transformation in the model of labor that can be periodized in terms of forty years of import-substitution industrialization, which culminates in 1970 with the Popular Unity government and the "structural adjustment," "shock treatment," and other economic reforms that have characterized the Chilean model of neoliberalism since the 1973 military coup. Both *Oír su voz* and *Mano de obra* represent this transformation in terms of the dedifferentiation of the spheres of human activity and the economization of life under neoliberalism. In this context work is not defined as a repetitive and predictable activity ruled by the logic of rationalization (the elimination of the qualitatively human, individual attributes of the worker), specialization (where work is reduced to the mechanical repetition of a set of actions), and calculability (the breakdown of complexity into its elements in order to predict with ever greater precision all possible results). Instead human capital's and post-Fordism's concepts of labor celebrate the blurring of the borders between work and action and the ability to maneuver in conditions of unforeseeablility, unpredictability, and undecidability; they privilege a vision of the new, linguistic performances, and virtuosity. These are the points of similarity between the two texts. The fundamental difference is that *Mano de obra*'s diagnosis and narrativization of this transformation present the emerging model of labor as an increasingly reifying process. Instead of offering sites of resistance to capital's latest regime of accumulation, the model of virtuoso labor appears in *Mano de obra*—and in contrast to the previous labor movements cited in the novel—as an intensification of the commodification of knowledge and action. Counterpointing Fontaine's and Eltit's visions of neoliberal labor reveals the shared logics that exist between human capital and post-Fordist immaterial labor. Eltit's emphasis on the latter as a form of subjection rather than as a producer of alternative subjectivities returns us to the opening scene of this chapter and that founding moment of Chilean neoliberal modernization, the union between violence and commodification. The novel suggests that the far-reaching consequences of this union require a move beyond a humanist critique of neoliberalism, which defends essentially human qualities that supposedly cannot be subsumed by the logic of supply and demand. It also puts into question the effectiveness of categories such as biopower versus biopolitics (where the former is conceived as the administration of life and the latter as the possibility of producing alternative subjectivities) for critically thinking about alternatives to neoliberalism's logic of dedifferentiation. The regime of domination that is represented in the novel, where the workplace is extended to all spheres of human action and where the differences between physical and intellectual labor have collapsed, calls for a reevaluation of the grounds of critique after this collapse.

3

RESTITUTION, MEMORY, AND THE MARKET

The Chilean Documentary

What Chile represented, after all, was a sort of twentieth-century Paris Commune.

—Patricio Guzmán, quoted in Anna M. Lopez, *The Battle of Chile*

Restitution, as a restoration to a previous state or as a giving of an equivalent for a past crime, is a politics marked by its own impossibility. This impossibility, which is firmly lodged in the very heart of the restitutional project, betrays its reparational efforts at every turn, constantly conjuring up the specter of the irreparable and the irredeemable. The latter confront the work of restitution with an impossible question: what scale, equivalence, or exchange (affective, economic, or otherwise) can be drawn upon to account for those historical wrongs that lie beyond measure? Writing on the relation between restitution and postdictatorship, Brett Levinson articulates the problem as a suspension of all conventions of measure: "Radical injustice, that is, emerges not when a crime is committed, and not when the law appears as insufficient and/or erroneous, but when every convention surfaces as obsolete—as pertaining to another time and place—and, therefore, every act of restitution as impossible."[1] A turn to a discussion of restitution is, I would argue, of particular relevance for the Chilean present. Fifteen years after the end of the dictatorship, the publication of the Valech Report in 2005 (a 1,200-page document that details the systemic torture committed during the seventeen-year

Pinochet dictatorship and proposes reparations for the victims) filled an important lacuna left by the 1991 National Truth and Reconciliation Report (which limited itself to reporting deaths and disappearances, not acts of torture) and the *Mesa de Dialogo*.[2] This historic publication, along with the official recognition and denouncement of the army's use of torture by General Juan Emilio Cheyre—the commander of the Chilean army at the time—and the human rights cases filed against the former dictator Augusto Pinochet, which followed him (along with charges of embezzlement and tax evasion) until his death in December 2006, renewed a long-standing national debate about the problems of redress, reparations, and restitution.

Building on the theoretical work on restitution advanced by Alberto Moreiras, Brett Levinson, and Patrick Dove, I begin by thinking about restitution as an impossibility not simply to demarcate a dead-end project but to propose the possibility of a restitutional thinking that avoids the now all-too-familiar pitfalls of melancholic angst, negotiated justice, and the politics of repentance in order to confront the implications of the unexchangeable singularity of loss. In this chapter I explore these problems through an analysis of one of the most notable cultural forms of the Chilean dictatorship and postdictatorship period: the social documentary.[3]

The Work of the Past: The Benjamin-Horkheimer Debate

In an exchange between Max Horkheimer and Walter Benjamin concerning the latter's essay "Eduard Fuchs, Collector and Historian," the question of whether the work of the past is complete is a point of contention. In the Fuchs essay—which explores, among other things, the essential elements of a materialist critique of works of art—Benjamin proposes that for historical materialism the work of the past is always incomplete. A work of art's prehistory undergoes constant change by virtue of its posthistory, and the work's effects encompass not just the encounter with the work of art but the entire history that has brought the work down to us. In a letter written in 1937, Horkheimer responds: "The pronouncement of incompleteness is idealistic if it does not incorporate completeness as well. Past injustice is done and finished. Those who have been beaten to death are truly dead. Ultimately you are making a theological statement. If one takes incompleteness absolutely seriously, then one must believe in the Last Judgment. My thinking is too contaminated with materialism for that."[4]

Benjamin's seminal essay the *Thesis on the Philosophy of History* counters Horkheimer's materialist objection by further developing the theological elements that are at the heart of his theorem on the incompleteness of the work of the past. Thus in the *Thesis,* Benjamin is responding not only to Horkheimer's materialist objections but also to Marx's claim in the "Eighteenth Brumaire" that for the social revolution of the nineteenth century, the notion of the incompleteness of the work of the past leads not to the glorification of the new struggles, but to farce. For Marx, "the tradition of all the dead generations weighs like a nightmare on the brain of the living"; hence the revolution cannot draw its strength from the past but must let "the dead bury their dead" and look toward the future.[5] As suggestive as Benjamin's redemptive criticism of Marxism is, the question remains: does his enlisting of theology create the conditions under which historical materialism can, like the chess-playing automaton, match each move of an opponent with a countermove? Can the work on memory politics—much of which is indebted to Benjamin's writings—exorcize the specter of the unexchangeable singularity of loss, which, as Horkheimer has noted, stubbornly haunts Benjamin's thinking about the incompleteness of the work of the past?

From the Incompleteness of the Work of the Past to the Politics of Memory

Benjamin's incompleteness of the work of the past is a point of entry to begin to think about a disparate group of discourses that make up what has come to be called "the politics of memory." Milan Kundera's often-cited reaction to the history of Communist Czechoslovakia, "the struggle of man against power is the struggle of memory against forgetting," is perhaps the field's most recognizable slogan.[6] Interrogating what is commonly meant by the phrase "the politics of memory," Jonathan Boyarin asks: "Is memory being understood here as a force that dictates a political situation? Or is it a distinct sphere of life that has its own political discourse?"[7] In his own work, Boyarin defines the politics of memory as the mobilization of the past for political purposes. This entails thinking about the past as not really past, but as a form of spatialized time that breaks with the model of a one-dimensional line moving through three-dimensional space. For this project Benjamin is central, for he understands the past to be a material resource the control of which is a key aspect of any political struggle. If one of the basic premises of the politics of memory is that the past needs to be conceived of as something that is constantly in dispute, then memory becomes a privileged field for political action because, in Benjamin's words, it is imbued with "a retroactive force that will constantly call into question every victory, past and present, of the ruler."[8] The politics of memory puts into question the completeness of the past by proposing that death is never past but always subject to the memory it is given through action in the present. To cite one well-known example, the transformation of the Puntas Carretas prison in Montevideo—which served as a torture center during the military regime—into a glittery, modern shopping mall undermines the notion that there is no safe "pastness" in death and supports Benjamin's thesis that "even the dead will not be safe from the enemy if he wins. And this enemy has not ceased to be victorious."[9]

Andreas Huyssen has put forward a more critical periodization of the politics of memory. He situates its most recent emergence as part of an epochal change that occurred in the 1980s: twentieth-century modernity's fixation on present futures has been replaced with a fixation on present pasts.[10] Huyssen includes as examples of this mnemonic shift the mass marketing of nostalgia; the phenomenon of musealization; the boom in memoirs, confessional literature, autobiography, and historical fiction; the emergence of trauma studies; and the proliferation of discussions regarding reparations for past injustices.[11] The question Huyssen's work on memory politics tries to answer is presented in a very economic form: why is the past selling better than the future right now? His answer takes the form of a "cultural logic of" argument where contemporary memory cultures are read as reaction formations of economic globalization.

For the purposes of this project, these general discussions regarding memory politics need to be thought through the specificity of the contemporary Chilean context. In an article on the politics of memory and political action in Chile, Lessie Jo Frazier attempts to isolate "resistant memories" capable of reinvoking contestatory politics in a time of neoliberal euphoria.[12] Frazier opposes this project, defined as the task of "countermourning" (a perpetually oppositional dialogue with the dead for the pursuit of justice), to the Freudian memory work of mourning, which she associates with the discourse of the now-governing coalition of democratic parties. Mourning, according to Frazier, is part of a state discourse that relies on a vocabulary of compromise, opportunity, advantage, and reconciliation in order to legitimate the neoliberal transition: "the vocabulary of mourning, as a tool for soothing grief in order to supersede it, accommodates neoliberal discourse."[13] Frazier's essay engages in the important work of denaturalizing the dichotomy that the Chilean social sciences have established between authoritarianism and the democratic transition. José Joaquín Brunner is a key figure in the constitution of this dichotomy, which subsumes everything that is opposed to authoritarianism into a liberal and democratic project. This is one of the legitimizing moves of the "transition to democracy" that, led by a coalition of political parties hegemonized by neoliberal forces, unquestioningly adopts the economic model imposed on the country during the military years. The Brunner essay that is most relevant for the purposes of this study is one where he describes a series of cultural practices that opposed the military dictatorship. Among these practices Brunner singles out the importance of memory: "The symbolic experience of democracy is transformed into the central axis of a collective memory."[14] This discourse interpellates popular memories that were articulated in a context of antidictatorship into a postdictatorial project of transition without taking into account how they might resist, transform, or reject such a project. In other words, the logic of the transition dictates that any opposition to the dictatorship is by definition liberal and democratic. Frazier questions both the naturalized opposition between authoritarianism and democracy and the incorporation of popular memories into the project of the transition to democracy by focusing on examples of "countermemory." These include the poetry of Guillermo Ross-Murray Lay-Kim, who attempts to establish a "subversion of memory" (a poetic discourse that expresses rage, betrayal, vengeance, and damnation) that confronts the official lexical field (i.e., the vocabulary of mourning), and funeral rituals in the north of Chile that have the dual function of lamenting the dead and providing a space for political critique against the state policies of reconciliation and the denial of justice.

On the basis of these examples, Frazier goes on to make the broader claim that the practices of countermourning, which represent the "resilience of a few" who "grope toward a politics that might alloy their memories' integrity with a vision for the future," constitute a counterhegemonic politics of memory capable of challenging the hegemony of the neoliberal transition.[15] The examples of "countermourning" that Frazier presents make it difficult to share in this optimism. Her articulation of memory as something resistant and subversive that can be thrown in the face of the neoliberal transition seems to nostalgically hark back to the epic function that memory had in the antidictatorial struggles. What is lacking, I would argue, is an engagement with the specific context and contours of postdictatorship.

One of the far-reaching consequences of the Chilean transition from a context of dictatorship to a context of postdictatorship is that the status of the *enemy* has become ever more ambiguous. The act of naming the enemy has become an uncertain one; it is no longer possible—as in Patricio Guzmán's 1975 documentary *The Battle of Chile,* when, with ominous music playing in the background, the camera pans over a group of conspiring generals, and a sign discerns them as "the bosses"—to easily identify a transcendent apparatus that imposes rule and order. Consequently, the oppositional strategies, counterdiscourses, and other paradigms of resistant agency that were effectively mobilized against the dictatorship have been faced with the following problem: how can resistance be articulated when the enemy has become seemingly invisible? Or when the mechanisms of social command seem to have become immanent to the social field and to extend well outside the structured sites of social institutions? Returning to the debate between Benjamin and Horkheimer, the productive tension between an active forgetting that lets the "dead bury their dead" and a memory politics whose strength is drawn from "the image of enslaved ancestors rather than that of liberated grandchildren" is potentially put into crisis by the mass-media saturation and "informationalization" of memory. In other words, one of the characteristics of postdictatorship Chile is that the boom in memory becomes undistinguishable from the boom in forgetting. Thus, the question of the mobilization of memory as a resource for political action and the problem of its saturation and subsumption into information need to be considered concurrently.

My thinking on the problems of memory begins with the premise that the "great transformation"—to echo Martínez and Díaz's resurrection of Polanyi's term for the Chilean transition from the hegemony of the state to the hegemony of the market—has estranged concepts and categories such as the nation, the people, sovereignty, and rights and rendered them incongruous to the present landscape. Emptied of the explicative or mobilizing power that they may have once deployed, they are now available only in their fallen condition, as ruins in which we take refuge—at least in any kind of unproblematic way—at our own peril.

Patricio Guzmán and the Chilean Documentary

The work of Patricio Guzmán (specifically the cycle of documentaries *The Battle of Chile, Memoria obstinada, The Pinochet Case,* and *Salvador Allende*) situates itself within the antagonistic space often represented by, on the one hand, Marx's claim that the revolution can only create its poetry from the future and, on the other, Benjamin's figure of the angel of history and his notion of the incompleteness of the work of the past. Equipo Tercer Año's *The Battle of Chile*—a three-part documentary that films the last ten months of the Popular Unity government, culminating with the military coup on September 1973—is generally recognized as one of the most ambitious documentaries produced in Latin America in the 1970s.[16] Its much-lauded testimonial power is often contrasted with that of another influential documentary of that period, the Argentinean Grupo Cine Liberación's *La hora de los hornos.* This contrast puts into tension the avant-garde and montage-based work of the latter film with the supposedly more direct, immediate, and informational cinema verité mode of *The Battle of Chile* (often characterized by its informational density, excessive detail, and lack of background information). This much-repeated distinction needs to be relativized, for it gives a false impression of Guzmán's documentary, whose filmic operations (the extensive use of sequence shots, which are the film's signature characteristic, and the use of pans, tilts, and manual cranes) are more akin to fictional rather than to conventional documentary filmmaking strategies.[17] Elements of Guzmán's documentary such as voiceover, flashback structure, and self-referential moments when the process of producing the film are included in the final product all contradict the ideas of "direct cinema" with which it is often associated, thus complicating the notion that one is watching history in the making. The documentary's very title—a direct allusion to Gillo Pontecorvo's 1967 film *The Battle of Algiers*—plays on this opposing internal dynamic. Following in the cinematic tradition of Sergei Eisenstein and inspired by Fanonian Third Worldism, Pontecorvo's film reenacts the Front de Libération Nationale's 1954 anticolonial struggle against the French in order to show how the Algerian defeat at the Battle of Algiers eventually led the way to the triumph of the Algerian Revolution (i.e., in the film the part stands for the whole). Undoubtedly, this idea of a future victory in the face of a momentary defeat is the principal connection that *The Battle of Chile* wishes to establish with *The Battle of Algiers* (although without the latter's benefit of historical hindsight), but there are other important similarities, such as the fact that both start at the end and flash back to the events that lead up to it (part 1 of *The Battle of Chile* begins with sounds of the bombing of the Chilean presidential palace, La Moneda, during the opening credits), and both represent attempts to film a collective protagonist.[18] A signally important difference is that the Pontecorvo film is in its entirety a dramatic reenactment; as the opening credits proclaim, it contains "not one foot" of newsreel or documentary film footage. Yet through the use of handheld cameras, frequent zooms, and long lenses, *The Battle of Algiers* recreates the style of mass-media reportage.

One of the reasons for this apparent contradiction between *The Battle of Chile*'s status as a documentary that shows history as it is unfolding and the fictional filmmaking strategies it employs is that the film documents the Grand March (the massive mobilizations in the streets and factories that characterized the Chilean transition to socialism during the Popular Unity period) and at the same time—in a kind of chronicle of a death foretold—documents the end of this historical protagonist in the wake of the military coup. Thus in this film—edited in its entirety in Cuba after the coup—we already see a reflection on the catastrophe, including the highlighting of the cataclysmic representational, linguistic, and ideological effects of the coup and exile.[19]

Memoria obstinada and the Interruption of Memory Politics

In 1996, twenty-three years after the military coup and the filming of the documentary *The Battle of Chile,* Patricio Guzmán returned to Chile with a copy of this documentary—which until that moment had not been shown publicly in Chile—in order to engage with the people who had appeared in it and to attempt to relate to those who were very young or not yet born at the time of the military coup. The latter project falls within the parameters of what in this chapter I have been calling the politics of memory. And more specifically, it belongs to what Marianne Hirsch has called the task of "postmemory" (which, of course, is an attempt not to go beyond memory politics but to extend them). According to Hirsch, *postmemory* refers to remembrances that are mediated not only through recollection but through a process of imaginative investment and invention; it is distinguished from memory proper by generational distance and from history by deep personal investment. Hence it refers to those who grow up dominated by powerful narratives that often precede their birth. Guzmán's 1997 documentary film could be characterized as being the result of this kind of engagement, and from this perspective its most ambitious gesture is to attempt to bridge the abyss between the always mediated memories of those who had firsthand experience of the events leading up to and following 11 September 1973 and second-generation remembrances, marked by the work of postmemory, that feed themselves on leftovers, fragments, and incomplete sources. In what follows I will analyze the strategies the film employs to advance this project, while at the same time revealing the contradictions and interruptions that ultimately undermine it. It is this latter critical move—the revelation of the limits of the politics of memory—that permits a glimpse of what lies beyond: a thinking of restitution.

One of the documentary's strategies for bridging generational distance is tapping into the "weak Messianic power" that the past claims of the present. Scenes that work to produce this effect include: the reenactment performed by Salvador Allende's surviving bodyguards of the president on parade; the marching band of young musicians who play "Venceremos," the anthem of Popular Unity, in present-day downtown Santiago; and the juxtaposition of black-and-white images of National Stadium in 1973, when it was converted into a concentration camp, with images of the confrontations that now take place there between police in riot gear and euphoric soccer fans. These examples are part of a strategy that refuses to present history as a progression through homogeneous, empty time and opts to fill the past with the presence of the now. This Benjaminian notion of how historical materialism breaks with historicism presents itself in the film as a way of advancing the debate around the politics of memory and the Chilean experience of the transition.

Another strategy for bridging the generational distance is the film's focus on the reception of, and subsequent dialogue and debate over, *The Battle of Chile* by a generation for whom, in many cases, the experience of the coup preceded their birth. It is in these scenes—where there is a higher degree of mediation between past and present and where the relationship with the past is more indirect and fragmentary—that the struggle between competing discourses and interpretations comes to a head with the most intensity. In one of the final scenes of *Memoria obstinada,* the attempt to bridge the memories of those who had firsthand experience of the events documented in the film and the second-generation remembrances of those watching the film takes a curious turn. *The Battle of Chile* is viewed by a group of students who are sympathetic to the Popular Unity government, and it evokes passionate discussion about the traumas of the past and the oblivion of the present. Present during this discussion is Ernesto Malbran, one of the protagonists who appeared in the film. His triumphant discourse, which seeks to "make whole what has been smashed" in order to remedy the distortions suffered under the dictatorship and postdictatorship regimes, clashes with the students' tentative, collaborative, and piecemeal reconstructions of the past. In this way the film produces its own moment of danger; its project of bridging generational memories is threatened because the readings of the past offered by the students are put into the perilous situation of being ideologically captured by Malbran's prepotent discourse.

The film's struggle to rescue *The Battle of Chile* both from its lack of circulation in Chile and from the ossifying forces of monumentalization is another way that *Memoria obstinada* attempts to establish a unique experience with the past. This struggle is an attempt to save *The Battle of Chile* from becoming a reified and static image of the past that inhabits future generations' memories like, in Marx's terms, "a nightmare on the brain of the living."[20] This project is undertaken by having the participants and protagonists of *The Battle of Chile* come together twenty-three years later in order to engage in the task of remembering, recuperating, and reinterpreting. In the case of Juan, one of the survivors of the bombing of the presidential palace La Moneda, footage of the bombing is intertwined with his personal biography and then juxtaposed with footage of a return visit to the rebuilt La Moneda; Ignacio Valenzuela, Jaime Guzmán's uncle, tells the story surrounding the documentary's escape and exile from Chile; Salvador Allende's former bodyguards reunite to identify and give personal testimony about their missing coworkers.

The choreographed performances that the documentary films, which are all related to the incompleteness of the work of the past, bring to the foreground the changing contexts and contours of postdictatorship. In this way, the film opens up a critical space for the examination of the Chilean transition. In this context I am using *transition* as a description not of a movement from one place to another (i.e., from the situation of dictatorship to postdictatorship) that necessarily implies the experience of revolution or change, but of movement without metamorphosis, as homogeneous, empty time. This particular notion of transition has been powerfully articulated in the work of the Chilean philosopher Willy Thayer: "It is likely that the distrust that surrounds the word 'transition' comes from our use of it—not innocently—to refer to a state of things where nothing transits nor is in the process of transiting. It is a state of things that we predict will not suffer any movement, or that has already transited definitively, and from this point on, its last transit, it will never transit again, threatening us with its definitive stay."[21] Thayer's work situates the dictatorship as transition in the strong sense of the term, as passage from the sovereignty of the state to the sovereignty of the market. He articulates it outside of the ideological registrar of the social sciences, freeing it from some ideological incrustations and permitting other kinds of connections and possible implications to be derived from it.[22] In other words, Thayer posits the challenge of reflecting on a transition emptied of the experience of revolution and change; it is a transition that names the neoliberal present as an intransitive and stationary reality.

Memoria obstinada can be understood as an attempt to take up this challenge and to break with this transition ideology by, once again in Benjaminian terms, blasting open the continuum of history and establishing a unique experience with the past. And yet, the apocalyptic overtones that are perceivable behind Thayer's notion of a definitive transition that already occurred call into question at every moment the possibility of such an undertaking. The unique experience with the past that Guzmán's documentary, through the different strategies and performances I have described, attempts to elicit is always tempered with a sense of estrangement. For example, the film juxtaposes 1970s footage of then-president Salvador Allende on parade in a slow-moving car surrounded by his bodyguards, waving to his cheering supporters who fill the streets, with a reenactment that Guzmán filmed more that twenty-three years later, with the surviving bodyguards around an empty car on a small and barren back street. It is as if the empowering moment, when the past is filled with the presence of the now, also reveals in an uncanny way a sense of irreparable loss. The film's most poignant moment emphasizes this sense of loss and casts a lingering doubt upon the feasibility, and even the legitimacy, of memory politics. The moment occurs when an image of a woman at a pro-Allende rally is picked out of the crowd and identified as Carmen Vivanco. When confronted with this image twenty-three years after it was filmed, Carmen Vivanco does not recognize herself: "Maybe it is . . . but I have my doubts," she responds to the interviewer.[23] One possible reading is that this is a symptom of the culture of fear, one of the legacies left over from years of military repression. But it can also be understood as a refusal to enter into the recuperative logics of the politics of memory; for Carmen Vivanco this black-and-white image, rather than bringing back the past and possibly capitalizing on it as a privileged field for political action, emphasizes the irreversible and irretrievable nature of the past. The distant and detached way in which she goes on to list the names of her family members who were disappeared during the dictatorship seems to suggests that, as Horkheimer puts it, "the injustice, the pain, the terror of the past are irreparable."[24] Vivanco ends up critically questioning one of the basic premises of the politics of memory by reinserting the notion of the completeness of the past into the discussion.

Returning to the counterpoint between *Memoria obstinada* and *The Battle of Chile:* the former, filmed twenty-three years later, works in a much more reflexive, nostalgic-melancholic register (opposed to other, more militantly heroic documentaries, such as Patricio Henriquez's *11 de Septiembre, 1973: el ultimo combate de Salvador Allende* and Miguel Littin's *Acta general de Chile: Miguel Littin clandestino en Chile*). By focusing principally on intimate stories of tragedy and loss, and including all the melancholy reenactment sequences, there appears to be an abandonment of the vocabulary of collective action and massive mobilization that marked Guzmán's earlier work. It has on this account been criticized by sectors of the left for being too in step with the atomization and dispersal of social life associated with free-market Chile (following what Bourdieu has called neoliberalism's systematic destruction of collectives). A case in point is the historian Thomas Miller Klubock's article on the alleged neoliberal passage from *The Battle of Chile* to *Memoria obstinada,* which offers a very blunt formulation of the above argument. He proposes that Guzmán is guilty of shifting the camera's focus from the social groups and movements central to the revolutionary process of the Popular Unity years to more intimate and individual experiences that induce nostalgia, loss, and melancholy. For Klubock, the main problem is that "the film's [*Memoria obstinada*'s] powerful evocation of personal tragedy and loss produces a sense of memory that is restricted to the individual and defined by nostalgia, rather than a form of collective memory engaged with current political questions."[25] The latter form of "collective memory," which Klubock champions, includes defending Popular Unity's socialist project; critiquing neoliberal policies; and confronting the legacy of human rights abuse by tapping into the work of the different human rights groups, grassroots organizations, labor groups, and historians (the reference here is to the document *Manifiesto de historiadores*) that have struggled, and continue to struggle, against the dictatorship's legacy.[26]

It is not true, as Klubock affirms, that in the documentary everything is driven inside and public spaces are not represented; in fact, as I have argued, the uncanny effect of restaging public performances in a radically transformed Chile is one of the most compelling aspects of Guzmán's documentary. It is true—and I believe this is what Klubock is attempting to signal—that *Memoria obstinada*'s public performances are the antithesis of the massive social movements filmed in *The Battle of Chile*. The performances produce a sense of estrangement and reveal, in an uncanny way, an irreparable loss, a loss that affects not only the reframed protagonists of *The Battle of Chile* but Chilean society as a whole. In this sense the estranging effect of the public performances corresponds more to the kind of gesture found in one of the paradigmatic texts of the postdictatorial scene: Eltit's national allegorizing of Chile through the figure of the schizophrenic and homeless Padre Mio: "It is a deep crisis of language, an infection of memory, a disarticulation of all ideologies. It is a shame, I thought. It is Chile, I thought."[27]

Although Klubock is right to point out the persistence of agents struggling for social change in postdictatorship Chile, the attempt to incorporate these diverse social forces under the banner of "collective memory" and place them within the historical narrative of the Grand March documented in *The Battle of Chile* threatens to empty these movements of their own historical specificity. Guzmán's critical potential lies precisely both in advancing an affirmative project of attempting to establish a unique experience with the past and—through the uncanny moments—in revealing the incommensurability and radical discontinuity between the two periods. Carlos Pérez Villalobos's analysis of *Memoria obstinada* moves in this direction. In one of the more interesting readings of Marx's "Brumaire," Pérez Villalobos affirms that situating this text in the present—what he refers to as "esta actualidad *post*"—turns it on its head. Marx's revolution-to-come, which served as the measure of whether an event was simply a farcical repetition or tragedy, has, according to Pérez Villalobos, already ensued. In the wake of the revolution, "all hope resides in conserving the memory of that which was lost and disappeared. Memory is the only possible syncopation that resists the confiscation of life by the market."[28] Thus, for Pérez Villalobos, in the wake of the neoliberal revolution, Guzmán's documentaries take on this historic mnemonic task.

One of the limitations of this kind of analysis is that in attempting to resuscitate memory politics in the wake of the revolution, it fails to register the tensions and contradictions that emerge in *Memoria obstinada*'s articulation of a politics of memory capable of intervening in the homogeneous, empty time of the transition. This, along with the attempts at isolating memory practices capable of reinvoking contestatory politics (such as those mobilized against the dictatorship), suggests the need to ground this kind of work in a deeper assessment of the epochal change that the dictatorship inaugurated. As I discussed earlier, a move in this direction would include Thayer's reworking the concept of transition so that it is no longer simply understood as the process of redemocratization that began with the 1988 plebiscite and continued with the political changes that have characterized the move from a military regime to a democratic one (elections, party politics, legislative debates, etc.). Thayer's notion of a transition that already occurred, as opposed to a transition that is stationary and intransitive, reveals that the epochal transition that Chilean society experienced was the military dictatorship and not the postdictatorial process of redemocratization. For it was the dictatorship that inaugurated the profound transition from the hegemony of the state to the hegemony of the market: "Transition names for 'us' not the transference of the dictatorship's governmental administration to a democracy, but rather the transformation of the economy and politics that the dictatorship enacted: the displacement of the state as the central subject of national history, to an excentric, poststate, and postnational market."[29] From the perspective of the transition as an epochal change that occurred during the dictatorship, the democratic reforms mentioned above have to a certain extent served as its legitimization by working within the political and economic parameters of a fiscally conservative state in an export-oriented, open-market society. The implications that this has for the study of a text like Guzmán's film is that it gets us beyond only seeing the derivative transition ("the transition to democracy"), and we can begin to discern some of the ramifications of more profound transformations. One of the consequences of this is that the particular notions of resistance and intervention that have been associated with the politics of memory need to be rearticulated in order to begin to address the situation of postdictatorship. This shift of emphasis, occasioned by the perspective of the transition as an epochal change carried out by the dictatorship, opens up the possibility of the further interrogation of a pressing set of questions, like the relationship between cultural production and the seemingly inevitable and irresistible character of neoliberalism, that have not been adequately addressed under the paradigm of memory politics.

Forensics and Restitution: *Anil's Ghost* and *Fernando ha vuelto*

In order to think about the role forensics plays in the project of critical restitution, I begin by briefly looking at Michael Ondaatje's 2000 novel *Anil's Ghost*. This is perhaps one of the most acute literary reflections on the enterprise of restituting what the novel refers to as "the unhistorical dead." The science of forensics is presented as the tool for bringing back into the light of history those who have been turned into ghosts through the work of state violence. After the torture, murder, and encryption of prisoners in nameless mass graves, the state's refusal to recognize the grievances of the families leaves their loved ones in a ghostly limbo. In the novel, the science of forensics appears on the scene as a way of intervening in this situation and possibly enabling a project of restitution.

Ondaatje's forensic thriller tells the story of Anil Tissera, a Sri Lankan émigré and forensic anthropologist. Working for a human rights organization, Anil returns to Sri Lanka, which has been plagued by twenty years of a three-tier war (a separatist insurrection, a leftist insurrection, and widespread government repression), to discover the skeletal remains of a victim of government violence. Armed with the discourse of the forensic sciences, Anil works to convert the partial remains of this body into identity markers: "Anil turned bodies into representatives of race and age and place."[30] The drive behind Anil's fervent restitutional mission—that is, the positive identification of skeletal remains—is twofold: the desire to save the body of a specific political prisoner from disappearing into the mass graves of the unhistorical dead and the desire, in so doing, to expose the government's dirty secret to the light of public scrutiny. This mission reveals the synecdochical logic that orients Anil's restitutional project: "To give him a name would name the rest."[31]

After setting up this restitutional project, the novel goes on to reveal its critical limits. It reveals the impossibility of a fully accomplished restitution, and then, at least on a certain level, it goes on to question its very desirability. As Sarath—Anil's companion throughout the novel—warns her, in war-torn Sri Lanka, searching for truth with an instrument that is simultaneously blunt and piercing, like the discourse of forensics, can be likened to putting "a flame against a sleeping lake of petro."[32] And ultimately, as her attempt to restitute the corpse of Sailor (the victim of government violence) ends up producing more corpses (Sarath's, among others), Anil discovers the limits of her own enterprise: "She used to believe that meaning allowed a person a door to escape grief and fear. But she saw that those who were slammed and stained by violence lost the power of language and logic."[33]

The forensic illusion of a fully accomplished restitution—similar to the Funes-like mnemonic fantasy of total recall—that is critiqued in the novel is contrasted with a parallel restitutional project: the work of Ananda, an artisan eye painter. Ananda artistically reconstructs the skeleton's face in order for the forensic team to be able to identify him. The problem is that—as part of a mourning process for his disappeared wife—Ananda ends up making Sailor's face look "peaceful." Beyond the exacting demands of Anil's restitutional project and its imperative to make the dead work for the living by bringing their bodies back to denounce government crimes, what Ananda "wants of the dead" after they have suffered so much violence and bloodshed is for them to finally look peaceful. In this sense, Ananda's work is closer to Marx's call to let the dead bury their dead than to a politics of memory.

The critique of the forensic project of restitution advanced in *Anil's Ghost* provides us with a critical introduction for discussion of another restitutional project where the discourse of forensics plays a central role: Silvio Caiozzi's documentary film *Fernando ha vuelto.* Caiozzi's documentary, which was shot in three days using two digital cameras, presents viewers with an important restitutional moment in the history of Chilean human rights: the identification and return of the remains of one of the disappeared to his family. The cadaver of Fernando Olivares Mori, a member of the leftist group Movimiento de Izquierda Revolucionaria (MIR) who was disappeared in 1973, had been exhumed from Patio 29 of the Cementario Nacional in Santiago and been under forensic investigation since 1991 (with the collaboration of family members) by a team of doctors and anthropologists at the Instituto Médico Legal. Seven years later, the documentary films the scene when the forensic technicians officially declare a positive identification of the remains of Fernando Olivares Mori and inform his widow, in meticulous detail, as to the causes of his death. It is a hauntingly jarring scene that makes visible the unassailable abyss between the restitutional demands of the family and what the factic, data-heavy discourse of forensics is able to offer. The detailed report accounting for every fracture and every blow leads the forensics team to 100 percent certainty about the identity and fate of Fernando Olivares. And as important as establishing the latter is, what is ultimately revealed is the extent to which the crimes that were committed lie beyond any measure. By presenting the ultimate restitutional scene—the return of Fernando's bones—the documentary makes visible the impossibility of alleviating the restitutional demand with the restoration of a particular object, monetary recompense, or even, as in this case, the singular weight of the victim's cadaver.

In his work on the articulation of restitution in Juan Rulfo's *Pedro Páramo,* Patrick Dove reminds us that restitution always points beyond: "the usurpation or re-appropriation of a good, a property or a right. The structure of this demand does not allow us to think that we will have alleviated its singular weight with the restoration of some particular: what is called for, we might hypothesize, is not just a symbolic restitution of a name, a title or a particular good, but instead an intervention in the symbolic domain itself."[34] And so it is to the documentary's intervention in this symbolic domain that we now turn. Frustrated by the material project of accomplished restitution, the documentary goes on to explore the possibilities of symbolic restitution. Despite the precision of the forensic analysis and the certainty with which it documents its findings, it runs up against what is now a familiar postdictatorial situation: if during the dictatorship the disappeared were treated as phantoms by the regime—again like in

Anil's Ghost, a case of the "unhistorical dead" that need restituting—now, at least in this case, where there exists material proof of the regime's acts of torture and the anonymous burial of Fernando Olivares, still nothing can be done. As one of the members of the forensic team puts it: "We have all the tests and proofs, but no one can do anything."[35] Another one of the forensic doctors rationalizes the effects of restitutional work as the possibility of producing a public document, a signed death certificate that "works for history, but not for justice."[36] In this way the restitutional project, represented by the figure of forensics, becomes, despite the materiality of its work, a form of symbolic intervention.

My aim here is not simply to repeat now-familiar critiques that have been leveled against other cultural texts such as *Memoria obstinada* (that it mimics a state discourse that relies on a vocabulary of compromise and reconciliation in order to legitimate the neoliberal transition). Nor do I agree with Carlos Pérez Villalobos's dismissal of *Fernando ha vuelto* as a depoliticizing text ("in Caiozzi's documentary the exhumation of Fernando's remains appears to stay on the side of a natural catastrophe, absent of all political content").[37] Instead, I want to focus on how the documentary ends up revealing the limits of its own restitutional project, how in the end it interrupts the cultural discourse of closure premised on the allegorized figure of forensics as a fully restitutional project.

After arriving at what seems to be a juridical impasse, the documentary leaves the cold, clinical space of the Instituto Médico Legal in order to focus on the family's private mourning rituals: the prayers around Fernando's bones, the sealing of the casket, the funeral procession to the cemetery, and the final lowering of the casket into the ground. This cultural work of closure, which in the documentary appears as work resigned principally to domestic spaces, is contrasted by Fernando's mother. Surrounded by pictures of her family taken before the catastrophe, and never having given up her lost object, she bears the heavy psychic scars of her pain. Having suffered through multiple strokes, she has all but lost the ability to make herself understood. Fernando's mother complicates one of the fundamental premises of the symbolic restitutional project; instead of "meaning allowing a person a door to escape grief and fear," she introduces Anil's challenge that "those who were slammed and stained by violence lost the power of language and logic." Instead of a symbolic fix, what we have here is a fissure at the very level of the symbolic order. It is a fissure that the documentary presents for each of its viewers, for ultimately what can one say in the face of such horror?

Similar to critical moments in *Memoria obstinada* such as Carmen Vivanco's refusal to enter into the recuperative logics of the politics of memory and one of the film's final scenes, where a student—overcome by the violent images on the screen—is unable to articulate a single word in response, Fernando's mother interrupts the documentary's attempt to create a cultural discourse of closure premised on the allegorized figure of forensics as a fully restitutional project. The latter is a restitutional project that purports to, in the words of the protagonist of *Anil's Ghost,* turn skeletal remains into identity markers ("representatives of race and age and place") in order to save the unhistorical dead from the oblivion of anonymous graves. Francine Maseillo's comments on *Fernando ha vuelto* seem to affirm the documentary's symbolic restitutional promise. She writes: "the materiality of the body (and what greater density could give expression to the body than its weight in bone?) was thus unmistakably claimed; bone and personal identity, past history and current moment were linked in a single image, joining the visual presence of the skeleton to the highly unrepresentable aspects of physical and emotional pain."[38] This reading of Caiozzi's documentary is in line with the general project Masiello develops in her book, which explores the possibilities of "artistic avenues of access through which a particular loss might help us make sense of a social whole."[39] In this rearticulation of the politics of memory, Masiello reaffirms the aesthetic dimension of such a project: "Art and literature thus force us to think of interpretative strategies of resistance, interrogating the past and leading to a politics of cognition with which to move toward the future."[40] Yet, as I have argued, imbuing the documentary with the fully restitutional task of "claiming the materiality of the body" or "joining the visual presence of the skeleton to the highly unrepresentable aspects of physical and emotional pain" ignores the documentary's productive work of revealing the limits of its own restitutional project. And in so doing, the documentary exceeds its own form as archive and information, pointing us toward an impossible restitution that lies beyond the purview of memory politics.

Restitution beyond Restitution

The discussion in this chapter has attempted to take up the challenge to memory politics posed by Alberto Moreiras: that is, his challenge to imagine "a new thinking beyond memory: a postmemorial thinking, aglobal, coming to us from the singularity that remains, residually."[41] In order to understand the implications of this call to thinking beyond memory, I turn to Moreiras's work on the problem of restitution, where he proposes the possibility of a metacritical outside to the appropriational and restitutional drives that have characterized Latin Americanism's relation to its singular object. Following Geoffrey Hartmann and Enrico Martí Santi's critique of how the work of restitution ends up subordinating the other to the self's salvational perspective (and ultimately functioning to ease the self's historical consciousness), Moreiras goes on to outline the possibility of a critical restitution, that is, a destabilizing force that offers an opening to alterity. Although in agreement with the latter thinkers that one of the limits of a fully accomplished restitutional thinking is that it both reduces and preserves alterity, Moreiras contends that this does not exhaust the possibilities of restitutional thinking and that what is at stake is the possibility of an opening to nonknowledge and the revelation of the excessive ground of Latin Americanism. Beyond a static and limiting notion of restitution as something that can be fully accomplished or achieved, one of the critical potentials in restitution that is identified by Moreiras is that it can look to its own point of closure in an attempt to come to the end of itself.

This thinking about restitution is of a wholly different order than more prevalent ones, such as Elazar Barkan's, which posit restitution as a novel form of politics based on the interactions between perpetrators of crimes and their victims in an effort to build an interpretation of the past that both parties can share. This latter pragmatic conceptualization of restitution, which aims to "negotiate justice so that it is politically feasible," empties it of its legal and economic qualities in order to focus on the cultural work of turning a traumatic experience into a constructive narrative of identity.[42]

On a superficial level both Guzmán's and Caiozzi's documentaries attempt a similar undertaking. Operating under the aegis of memory politics, they attempt to develop a salvational vocabulary based on a static notion of accomplished restitution. The former documentary attempts to do this by tapping into an epic (antidictatorial as opposed to postdictatorial) notion of memory, and the latter tries to articulate a cultural discourse of closure premised on the allegorized figure of forensics as a fully restitutional project.

Patricio Guzmán's 2004 film *Salvador Allende* is another example of an attempt to restitute the past. It continues exploring issues of memory, erasure, and the transformation of Chile since the coup, but this time focusing on the figure of Salvador Allende. Beginning with a shot of the only surviving material remains of Allende—a wallet with some banknotes, his Socialist Party membership card, a watch, an initialed leather case, a sash, and a shattered fragment of his signature black glasses—the film attempts to make whole what has been smashed by exploring who Allende was and why he had such a profound effect on Chilean history. The phrase that is repeated throughout the documentary, "the past does not pass" ("el pasado no pasa"), firmly situates the film within a Benjaminian framework regarding the incompleteness of the work of the past. The film struggles to—as Volodia Teitelboim, one of the people interviewed, puts it—recuperate Allende. This recuperation works against the silences of the past, the vilification of Allende by the right, and some of the heroic monumentalizations of Allende by the left.

The tone of the film is even more intimate, personal, and autobiographical than *Memoria obstinada.* In his narration, Guzmán explains that one of the motivations for the film was the realization that Allende had been one of the people who had most influenced his life. "I would not be who I am," the narrator tells us, if Allende had not embarked on the project that led to Popular Unity. And yet, Guzmán goes on to say, the first time he sees Allende he ignores him. Similarly, his epic documentary, *The Battle of Chile,* is not a film about Allende. Allende appears in sections of the film, because he formed part of the historical scene being filmed, but the protagonist of *The Battle of Chile* is a collective subject, *el pueblo.* One of the great contributions of the documentary is producing a visual representation of this collective subject. In terms of the kind of analysis advanced and the problems explored, *Salvador Allende* is much closer to *The Battle of Chile* than to *Memoria obstinada*. The latter focuses on the transformations Chilean society underwent after the military coup and the dictatorship, whereas *Salvador Allende* and *The Battle of Chile* focus more on understanding the Popular Unity period (1970–73) and the forces that led to the military coup. And yet these last two documentaries offer very different perspectives on this period. One of the very dynamic characteristics of *The Battle of Chile* is that the documentary struggles to find a form that is capable of representing the historical period that it is documenting. The period leading up to the 1973 military coup is one that is strongly marked by social division, antagonism, and polarization. As Ana Lopez has convincingly argued, *The Battle of Chile* reflects these social conflicts not only on the level of content but through the tensions it maintains between direct, unmediated representation and dramatized, thoroughly mediated representation.[43] *Salvador Allende* has a very different relation to its present. In a revealing narrative moment, Guzmán describes his relation to present-day Chile as that of a stranger in a hostile environment; the country is described as a cold, alien place whose values are connected to money and commerce. In contrast, the scene that follows cuts to an interview discussing the Popular Unity period as the country's most beautiful epoch. Not having a strong investment in the present, *Salvador Allende*'s representation of the Popular Unity period is also different from what is shown in *The Battle of Chile,* even though it is working with much of the same visual material. The tensions, divisions, and antagonisms that make up *The Battle of Chile* take a backseat in the later documentary, which gives a more straightforward account of the Grand March. The internal conflicts, international pressures, and interventions serve as a foil to the power of Allende's personality, whose support is shown to continue to grow in the face of all these obstacles. In this way the documentary project of symbolically restituting the figure of Allende from the fragments that remain, a project that takes on the challenges of the incompleteness of the work of the past, ends up distanced and removed from the problems of the present, rather than opening up new engagements with it.

The difficulty, as I argued at the beginning of this chapter, is that the "great transformation" (Chile's neoliberal transition) has estranged concepts such as memory politics, restitution, and the incompleteness of the work of the past. It has made them incongruous to the present landscape. Ultimately, this is what the documentaries reveal. The project of memory politics that they deploy reveals its own limits. And yet their critical potential is not exhausted in this negative critique, for what begins to emerge is the beginning of a thinking beyond memory politics and a vocabulary that abandons categories such as apology, forgiveness, and repentance, which have for too long established an untenable compromise between ethics and law. The challenge we are left with then is not simply to abandon the restitutional gesture, but to understand it as at once excessive and lacking, as both absolutely necessary and impossible. In this way what is ultimately interrupted is the containment, in documentary memory, of the coup as simply a horrible aberration, a barbaric hiatus, within an otherwise fluid continuum (democratic, modernizing, developing, etc.). This opening of the documentary archive is an opportunity to continue to explore the profound transformative effects of the coup and its transition.

4

CRITICAL VISUALITY OR GLOBAL SUBSUMPTION?

Neoliberal Biopolitics, Chilean Visual Arts, and the Economic Text

> There is something that is even more unsettling than the malaise of subjectivity in the anonymity of capital: the anonymous life of capital in the hidden fragments of each subjectivity.
>
> [Hay algo más tenebroso aun que el malestar de la subjetividad en el anonimato del capital, esto es: la vida anónima del capital en los fragmentos más recónditos de cada subjetividad.]
>
> —Federico Galende, "Diagnosticos de época"

Neoliberalism is too often invoked as either the explanation or the problem, as something that has exhausted itself or that has been all too triumphant. It is for this project precisely what remains to be explained. Taking a cue from the work that Michel Foucault began to explore in his 1978 seminar on neoliberal governmentality, where he focuses specifically on the postwar German Freiburg School and the Chicago School of Economics (Milton Friedman, George Stigler, and Gary Becker, among others), and Giorgio Agamben's work on bare life and the concentration camp, I examine the intimate relation between neoliberalism and biopolitics in the case of contemporary Chile.[1]

For the Chilean case, the focus on the Chicago School of Economics is, of course, by no means an arbitrary one. As I explore in chapter 2 in relation to the concept of human capital, it directly and symbolically impacted the Chilean economy and Chilean politics after the 1973 coup (directly, with the adoption of its economic reforms and the presence of economic advisors who studied there, and symbolically, as Milton Friedman's speech in Santiago following 11 September 1973 attests).

The counterpoint Foucault establishes between the forms of neoliberalism theorized by the German postwar Freiburg liberals and the Chicago School economists is instructive because it highlights just how radical the latter's proposal actually is. According to Foucault, the Freiburg liberals have an antinaturalist notion of the market: it is not a natural economic reality with intrinsic laws, but rather is constituted and maintained by constant political intervention. Within this scheme "pure competition" never naturally—or even fully—occurs; instead there is the sense of the market as an incessant and active politics. As a consequence there is not a negative conception of the state, where the state and the market are juxtaposed, but rather the one mutually presumes the existence of the other. Within this framework the economy is not a domain of autonomous rules and laws, but a space of constant social intervention and political regulation. Neither is there an all-determining logic of capital, but rather an economic-institutional entity that is historically open and can be changed politically. Thus, the difference between the Freiburg liberals and classic eighteenth-century liberalism is that the former propose that massive state intervention is necessary to anchor the entrepreneurial form. This gives the state/market relation a different valence: the Freiburg liberals want a state created on the basis of economic liberty (a form of sovereignty limited to guaranteeing economic activity) instead of, as is the case in the philosophy of Adam Smith, limiting the state in order to establish economic liberty.

The Chicago School proposes something else: the expansion of the economic form so that it applies to the totality of the social sphere, thus eliding any difference between the economy and the social. To quote Foucault's now-famous phrase at the end of his article "The Birth of Biopolitics": "American neoliberalism seeks . . . to extend the rationality of the market, the schemes of analysis it proposes, and the decision-making criteria it suggests to areas that are not exclusively or not primarily economic."[2] Thus economic analytical schemata and the criteria for economic decision making are applied to spheres of life that are not exclusively economic. What this represents is a transition from trying to govern society in the name of the economy (the project of the Freiburg liberals) to redefining the social sphere as an economic domain. The economy is no longer considered one social domain among others, but an area that embraces the entirety of human action. As a result, rational economic action becomes the all-encompassing principle of legitimation.

To reiterate, Foucault signals two principal differences between classical liberalism and neoliberalism: the redefinition of the relation between the state and the economy, where the market becomes the organizing and regulative principle; and the emergence of the figure *Homo economicus* as a central point of reference and legitimation. By encoding the social domain as an economic domain, cost-benefit analysis and market criteria can be applied to all instances of decision making. Thus the notion of natural freedom, which was the ultimate ground of classical liberalism, is replaced by the idea of economic liberty (the entrepreneurial and competitive behavior of economic-rational individuals). One question that Foucault raises is whether the neoliberal technologies of the self replace or produce the transition from state to market or whether specialized state apparatuses of regulation and control can coexist with these technologies of the self that encourage individuals to give their lives a specific entrepreneurial form (the idea being that the solutions to society's ills have less to do with social-structural factors and are more oriented to individual-subjective categories). From this perspective, neoliberalism is a political rationality that renders the social economic and links a reduction in state services to the call for "personal responsibility" and "self-care."

I take Gary Becker, Milton Friedman's most radical student and a Nobel Prize–winning economist, as the exemplary thinker of neoliberal biopolitics. According to Becker: "My research uses the economic approach to analyze social issues that range beyond those usually considered by economists."[3] The main axiom that guides his work is that all actors in the social game are rational agents who maximize their advantages in different cost situations. From this axiom he has gone on to consider such diverse issues as racial and sexual discrimination in labor markets, the investment in human capital, crime and punishment, marriage and divorce, the quantity and quality of children, and drug addiction, among others. As Becker puts it: "Decisions about the allocation of a consumer's non-market time and decisions about his choice of religion, marriage mate, family size, divorce, political party, or 'lifestyle' all involve the allocation of scarce resources among competing ends."[4]

To understand some of the implications of this approach, Becker's work on criminality is exemplary. He eschews all psychological, biological, or anthropological explanations of crime and establishes criminal activity as rational economic action: individuals become criminals because of the financial and other rewards they receive from crime compared to the rewards they might receive from legal work. This is decided by taking into account the likelihood of getting caught and convicted and the severity of the punishment. Seen from this neoliberal perspective, what is more effective, in terms of deterrence, is the probability of conviction rather than the severity of the punishment. Following this logic, Becker concludes that fines are a more efficient and effective form of deterrence than imprisonment. This line of reasoning leads to an interesting discussion regarding the possibility of thinking about theft as a redistribution of resources. Ultimately Becker decides it is not the latter because the time spent planning crimes is socially unproductive: it doesn't create wealth but only forcibly redistributes it.

In summary, from a neoliberal perspective the criminal is a rational-economic individual who invests, expects a certain profit, and risks making a loss. Crime is neither moralized nor seen as something that needs to necessarily be eliminated (at least not entirely); it is instead another market model among others. The supply of crime can be limited by negative demand, but it shouldn't be eliminated altogether. Instead the neoliberal project seeks to create neither a disciplining nor a normalizing society, but rather a society characterized by the cultivation and optimization of difference. Neoliberalism works as a difference engine. Unlimited conformity is considered detrimental to the system because a certain degree of criminality is good for the market (it all boils down to properly regulating its distribution).

Similarly with discrimination: Becker doesn't take a color-blind approach to the employee/employer/consumer relationship. From a neoliberal perspective, things can't be reduced to a value-neutral discourse about the productivity of workers. Becker takes into account discrimination coefficients (race, gender, and class) and speculates about situations when discrimination against a minority economically hurts the majority and when it doesn't (how much profit or wages they forfeit to avoid hiring or working with a minority or on the side of the consumer, how much more they are willing to pay for their discrimination).

The question is: what kind of groundwork or previous biopolitical work needs to be in place for this notion of economic totality to take such a firm hold in the modern imaginary? In other words, what are the necessary preconditions for the development of Chilean neoliberal biopolitics? The obvious answer is the fascist biopolitics advanced after the coup. But as I will argue, what needs to be better developed is the intimate relation between the two. It is at this juncture that Giorgio Agamben's work on the inner solidarity between the biopolitics of modern totalitarianism and the society of mass consumerism is particularly illuminating for understanding the Chilean experience.

From *Homo Economicus* to *Homo Sacer*

Agamben offers a corrective reading of the two figures he deems to be the principal thinkers of modern biopolitics: Michel Foucault and Hannah Arendt. Arendt he criticizes for not taking into account the biopolitical dimension of totalitarianism: she limits herself to describing the concentration camp as a laboratory of total domination. Foucault is critiqued for not including in his work on the exemplary sites of biopolitics (prisons and hospitals) the twentieth-century totalitarian state and, more specifically, the concentration camp. For Agamben, the camp is the most absolute biopolitical space: it is a space where power confronts biological life without any mediation, producing a zone of indeterminacy where bare life and political life become indistinguishable. Agamben makes the claim that the camp marks the political space of modernity and the emergence of a new political subjectivity: *Homo sacer.* There are some problems with this claim. Even though Agamben mentions the Spanish concentration camps in Cuba in 1896 and the concentration camps into which the English herded the Boers in 1899, his almost exclusive focus on Auschwitz results in a very short historical vision of modernity. The sweeping and general nature of the claims he is making points to the need to put the modern experience of the concentration camp in relation to the aforementioned colonial camp experiences.

I want to think about the birth of a fascist biopolitics through the case of the Chilean concentration-camp experience. The Chilean *testimonio Tejas verdes* is the fundamental text for understanding the birth of a fascist biopolitics (the emergence of *Homo sacer*) that violently lays the groundwork for, but is then intensified and surpassed by, neoliberal biopolitics (the emergence of *Homo economicus*).

For Agamben, using Foucault as a starting point, politics turns into biopolitics when natural life is included within the machinery of state power, and the distinction between the home and the polis, zoē and bios, natural life and political life, is obliterated. This transformation is what Foucault evokes with his often-cited phrase that at the threshold of the modern age, life is what is at stake in politics.[5] Agamben asks, what is the point where Foucault's double bind—the work of political technologies and the work of technologies of the self—converges? In other words, when does the seemingly voluntary servitude of individuals come into contact with objective power? Going even further, Agamben questions the possibility of maintaining these two (subjective technologies and political techniques) apart. Agamben's correction of Foucault can be formulated in the following way: the transitional moment of politics transforming into biopolitics (when "life is what is at stake in power") is not simply the inclusion of natural life into the polis, but rather the moment when bare life begins to coincide with the political realm, and "exclusion and inclusion, outside and inside, bios and zoē, right and fact, enter into a zone of irreducible indistinction."[6] Hence, bare life is simultaneously excluded from and captured within the political order. The sovereign is both inside and outside the juridical order: he has the legal power to suspend the law and therefore legally places himself outside of it. For Agamben this paradox marks the limit of the juridical order. The relation of exception is the capacity to include what is outside not by an interdiction or by an internment, but by suspending the juridical order's validity; it is an extreme form of relation by which something is included through its exclusion. The state of exception creates a zone of indistinction between inside and outside, between chaos and order.

Consequently, for Agamben the concentration camp—not the prison (for penal law is not outside the normal order) or the hospital—is the most absolute biopolitical space. It is the space of the exception (founded by martial law and the state of siege) that exists outside the normal juridical order, but it is not simply an external space. It is the privileged site of the production of bare life, what Agamben calls a life that may be killed and yet not sacrificed—that is to say, a life that is included in the juridical order solely in the form of its exclusion (its capacity to be killed).

Perhaps the most powerful and nuanced Chilean text regarding the process of being stripped of political status and reduced to bare life is Hernan Valdés's 1974 *Tejas verdes, Diario de un campo de concentración de Chile*. The critical attention this *testimonio* has received is not, as one might expect, because it is exemplary of dictatorial testimonial writing. When contrasted with this corpus of texts, what is striking are its idiosyncrasies and its unique vision of the concentration-camp experience. This is not to say that it doesn't contain the important characteristics normally associated with the dictatorial *testimonio* genre (documenting what happened, denouncing repression, accusing the perpetrators, and inspiring networks of solidarity). What distinguishes it from other *testimonios* is the profound sense of defeat it communicates, its near lack of heroism or articulation of resistance in the face of the advance of fascism. The text begins with a description of what Valdés calls "dead time" (waiting for passports, for the opportunity to flee, for the disappearance of friends, for the police to come), so that even before relating the concentration-camp experience, the narrator expresses a notion of desolation and collective defeat: "we were survivors of dead projects, of broken feelings."[7] The coup has disrupted all relationships; in the *testimonio* only precarious and obsessive ones are possible. Instead of providing a resistance-and-survival narrative, Valdés explores the penetrating and devastating effects of fascist technologies: how they inhabit and colonize his deepest and most secretive recesses, showing how no boundary—physical, psychological, or affective—holds up to this assault. This element of the testimonial has been best described by Ariel Dorfman as the difference between the militant witness, whose testimony enters the public sphere to reinforce the notion that there is a boundary beyond which barbarism cannot cross, and a text such as Valdés's, where the horror of fascism is that it does not find any final, inner barriers that successfully resist its dehumanization.[8] *Tejas verdes* moves testimonial writing from a description of the technologies of fascism to a reflection on their profound and enduring effects. It reveals another dimension of fascist horror that is not easily transformed into something to mobilize against. In moments of political urgency it is often passed over, for it voices that which no one wants to hear and is summarily dismissed as politically debilitating, counterrevolutionary, or irresponsibly self-indulgent. But what it does is change the focus from a position of outrage that such heinous crimes could possibly occur in a country like Chile to an exploration of the kind of deployment of power that reduces human beings to bare life and has rendered, at least until very recently, any acts committed against this life as noncriminal. To this day those implicated in the practice of torture and extermination insist that they did nothing except execute the word of the sovereign as law.

Both Karl Löwith and Hannah Arendt identify the total politicization of life as one of the fundamental characteristics of totalitarian states. Aspects of life that were once deemed private or neutral are subsumed in a political sphere that seems to have no boundaries. This is made manifest in Valdés as his obsession with discovering why he was taken prisoner transforms all his daily activities (eating habits, sleeping habits, idle conversations with neighbors, where he buys his bread and drinks his coffee) into indicators of a conspiratorial network. This politicization has a counterintuitive effect among the prisoners in the camp. The *testimonio* reveals no real sense of collective solidarity that grows among them. There is no discussion or analysis of the changes the country is suffering; instead there are discussions about individual bad luck, a distancing from political convictions and political parties: "In any case, it seemed that since we could not assume, or were not permitted to assume, all our potential political responsibility in those last three years, now, as if in revenge, we will deny responsibility for the failure, we will not embody it."[9] The group is reduced to, "in the best case, isolated individuals, occupied with maintaining our lives. Melancholic about what we could not do with history."[10]

Reading Valdés through the figure of *Homo sacer,* he appears as someone who through the concentration-camp experience is thrown into an indeterminate space founded by the military coup. It is indeterminate in the sense that it exists outside the juridical order but is not external to it (juridical law having been suspended through an act of the sovereign). The result is that in the *testimonio* Valdés's existence is reduced to bare life: he is stripped of every right by the fact that he can be killed without it being considered homicide (in Agamben's words, he can be killed but not sacrificed). Faced with the total politicization of life and the disarticulation of political militancy and solidarity, the narrator's only recourse to save himself is perpetual flight. The *testimonio* ends with Valdés's release from the concentration camp: "I get going, without looking where the Spaniard has gone, without looking back to observe the truck, which left immediately, I move faster and faster, without looking back, without seeing anyone, dizzy because of the space in front of me—it is an unfamiliar street—, I move in all haste, controlling myself in order to keep from running and to not turn my head around."[11] It is clear that in this perpetual flight he remains in continuous relationship with the power that banished him (the threat not to look back). His reincorporation into the polis does not shelter him from the threat of death; the city is now a strange and dizzying place, empty of familiar faces or reference points. It is in this sense that there is no possible return from the camp to something like "the home" or a return to the realm of classical politics. And it is from this biopolitical place, with its state of exception, total politicization of life, and systematic destruction of collectives, that subsequent biopolitical regimes need to be thought. The connection between neoliberal biopolitics and the fascist biopolitics associated with the concentration camp is further explored in Catalina Parra's visual-arts project. Parra takes strategies she developed in an antidictatorship context and adapts them to critique a new global economic order.

Setting the Scene: Visual Arts and Dictatorship in Chile

The *escena de avanzada,* a term advanced by Nelly Richard in her influential book *Margins and Institutions,* corresponds to a segment of the artistic and critical production that circulated during the dictatorship years. A diverse number of artists and thinkers are generally assembled under this term, including Carlos Altamirano, Roser Bru, Juan Castillo, Eugenio Dittborn, Diamela Eltit, Carlos Gallardo, Carlos Leppe, Gonzalo Mezza, Catalina Parra, Ximena Prieto, Lotty Rosenfeld, Francisco Smythe, and Raúl Zurita.[12] The critical literature on the Avanzada has generally situated its work in relation to three frames of reference: in contrast to the Chilean art scene during Popular Unity (marked by a commitment to the ideal of art for the masses, muralism, and engraved serialized images); in the wake of the violence and institutional destruction effected by the military coup; and foreclosed by the return of the major exile figures (many of whom criticized the Avanzada's rupturist vanguardist strategies) and the subsequent generation of young artists who turned away from Avanzada aesthetics in order to reclaim an aesthetics of the pictorial.[13]

Some of the general commonalities that give a sense of coherence to the Avanzada interventions and performances include the vanguardist strategies of quotation, cut-ups, montage, and collage; an incorporation and critique of the photographic register (here one would have to mention Carlos Leppe's work that focuses on the mutilation of the body as a violence done to portraiture, Roser Bru's figures of death and erasure, Eugenio Dittborn's images of lost identity buried in official files, and Catalina Parra's *imbunches*); an attempt to recreate notions of art and community as a way of countering the dictatorial eclipse of public spaces (the best examples being the art actions by the collective CADA, including the *NO +* artwork on city walls and the 1981 action *¡Ay Sudamérica!* where leaflets were dropped over poor neighborhoods in Santiago); and a vindication of the marginal as a place from which to advance the project of resignifying the social system.[14] According to Nelly Richard: "The coining of the term *Escena de Avanzada* sought to: (1) highlight the precursor of a combatative work with art and about art that participated in the avant-garde spirit of *formal experimentation and the politicization of the aesthetic;* (2) create a distance from the modernist epic narrative about the avant-garde that internationalizes the histories of metropolitan art, emphasizing rather the *local specificity of a scene of emergence.*"[15] Because of the conditions out of which they arose—dictatorial censure, lack of institutional support, and the lack of a critical language on the part of mainstream art critics and art publications with which to comment on them—Avanzada artworks tend to fuse text and commentary, creating what Richard has called a "politics of inscription." As a result, the Avanzada's sphere of influence transcended the field of visual arts and had an important impact on the literature, theory, and philosophy of the time.[16]

Ana María Dopico's project of establishing a relation between what she describes as José Donoso's "negative aesthetic dialectics" and Catalina Parra's neo-avant-garde visual arts strategies is an important precursor to the following discussion. Dopico focuses on Donoso's *Obsceno pájaro de la noche* as a limit text for critical interpretation. The novel offers, she claims, an untapped alternative to the "export economy of magical realism" and a radical critique of some of the more familiar tropes of the Latin American boom novel: miscegenational unions, emancipation through writing, the cultural memory of *nanas,* and adopted cultures.[17] Against this mainstream boom project, Dopico attempts to rescue Donoso's negative aesthetics—which for her reveal the wretched foundations underlying these more exportable forms—as the writing of those who are "exiled from the enticing mirages of peripheral capitalism, and from the auto-inscriptions and global market of 'national allegories.' It rests at the realm of the wretched that Fanon describes, not to rescue or enfranchise, but as a kind of nightmare capable of haunting the both Left and Right romances about Latin America during the Cold War."[18] Interestingly, Dopico offers an inverted version of Cornejo Polar's take on *El obsceno pájaro de la noche.* As I argue in chapter 1, Cornejo Polar issues a warning to future generations of writers and critics that they need to renounce the apocalyptic and nihilist tendencies espoused by Donoso in order to reconnect with history. For Dopico, on the other hand, Donoso's novel is an experimental model that offers the possibility for alternative and critical artistic practices in Latin America. She sees in the novel a refractory aesthetic that is inassimilable by the totalizing logic of the state, the dictatorship, or the market.

Catalina Parra's visual project then becomes, for Dopico, an example of how future generations take up Donoso's negative aesthetics. Parra's first exhibition in Santiago, at the Galería Epoca in 1977, was *Catalina Parra: Imbunches* (Ronald Kay and Eugenio Dittborn collaborated on this project).[19] Although it never made explicit references to the military repression of the period, the exhibition was filled with images of wounded people undergoing medical procedures, hospitals, body bags, and a map of Chile covered in gauze. It included barely veiled references to the disappeared, such as *Diariamente,* a montage that sewed together clippings (mostly obituaries) and images taken from *El Mercurio.* The newspaper clippings are molded into a loaf of bread (the bread that one consumes every day). The daily consumption of news and bread, along with the very word *diariamente,* is interrupted by a sharp tear containing shadowy figures hand-stitched into place with thick black thread, which elicits another kind of daily occurrence: the political disappearances that were not being reported by the news media. In another example, the photomontage *Coffin Capacity: One Person,* Catalina Parra resignifies Nicanor Parra's *artefacto* (the title of the work) by combining it with photographs of holes dug for cable lines in Germany. The effect is an oblique but powerful connection to the unidentified mass graves in Chile.

As a way of marking the problem of speaking pain and suffering, Parra used the figure of the *imbunche* (from the Mapuche story that tells of a creature whose bodily orifices have been sewn shut by witches to prevent the suspected evil from expressing itself). Among the reconstructions that made up this exhibit, Parra included passages from Donoso's *El obsceno pájaro de la noche:* "The *imbunche.* All sewed up, eyes, mouth, ass, genitals, nose, ears, hands, legs."[20] For Parra the *imbunche* (and specifically the Donosian version of it) functions as the muted narrative of enslavement, repression, and violent punishment. It becomes the figure of a nightmarish modernity driven by the dictatorship, producing sutured, mutilated, and censored bodies in its wake. It is in this sense that the dystopic figures evoked in Donoso's novel become material for future generations to return to in order to transform and redeploy them (in this case translated from the novel form to the art exhibition) at a moment when those dystopic figures have been intensified by the dictatorship. For example, similarly to the newspaper that lines the servants' room in *El obsceno pájaro de la noche* (newspapers that conjure up outdated events and forgotten catastrophes), Parra makes an *imbunche* out of a stack of copies of the Chilean newspaper *El Mercurio* (sewing the ends closed and bolting them together in Plexiglass), thus playing off the absolute transparency of the glass and the sutured evil that constitutes one of the most powerful symbols of official discourse in Chile. This initial engagement with Donoso's figure of the *imbunche* will mark all of Parra's future work; that is, the practice of sewing, stitching, and suturing images and text to the structure is one of her signature strategies.

There is no doubt that an explicit relation between Parra's work and Donoso's novel exists. The difficulty resides in situating Parra's work within the kind of alternative boom genealogy that Dopico attempts to establish via Donoso's novel. This is especially true if a longer view of Donoso's work is taken into account—one that doesn't just concentrate on *El obsceno pájaro*—for it puts such a genealogy into question. The distinction put into play between a consumable boom novel characterized by a replicative narrative virtuosity (Gabriel García Márquez is the obvious referent here) that Dopico opposes to a refractory novel whose experiments in radical critique end up breaking the novel form does not hold up to scrutiny. As I argue in chapter 1, situated within Donoso's larger narrative project, *El obsceno pájaro de la noche* marks both the maximum expression of late modernist boom aesthetics and its exhaustion.[21] The challenge in Donoso's case lies not, as Dopico argues, in returning to *El obsceno pájaro de la noche* in order to claim it in the name of a postmodern vanguard that "yielded both code and theory for a generation of writers and artists struggling to speak from within Chile's military dictatorship."[22] The challenge—one that Donoso's own later writing fails to live up to—is laid out in the Donoso novel that most directly deals with the military coup, *Casa de campo,* and is later satirized in *El jardín de al lado:* that is, what kind of writing is possible after the 1973 military coup, the collapse of the national popular project and its national allegorical narratives, and the neoliberal transformation of Chile (a transformation that I describe above as being based on the intimate relation between *Homo sacer* and *Homo economicus*)?

From this perspective the decidedly antimodernist gesture of returning to a seemingly outmoded modernist text (*El obsceno pájaro*) as a way of understanding contemporary aesthetic challenges (e.g., Catalina Parra's) to the epochal transformations inaugurated by the military coup doesn't take on the full magnitude of these transformations. Ultimately what is being prized in this return to *El obsceno pájaro de la noche* is its obscurity, its ability to articulate a critique that isn't registered by the repressive state forces and censors. Dopico concludes: "Deploying his [Donoso's] nightmares, Parra's generation developed a highly articulate and theoretical challenge to the politics of repression, one which still defines a Latin American cultural field grappling with the aftermath of violence and loss, and swimming against the tide of a global market."[23] It is the last line that interests me most, for it implies that the strategies developed against a repressive military state (the "theoretical challenge to the politics of repression") are also viable against an encroaching global market. It is with this problem in mind that I now turn to the later work of Catalina Parra.

Although the 1977 exhibit at the Galeria Epoca is Catalina Parra's most well-known and widely reviewed show, it is her later work on the problems of consumption, debt, and the saturation of the image in contemporary culture that are central to this book project. For it is in this later work that the *imbunche* sewing practices that were born out of the experience of the coup are moved out of the context of the dictatorship (with all its problems of censure, repression, and silence) and squarely put into the new global economic order. This transition in her work is mirrored by the abandonment of *El Mercurio* as the primary source of print material for her work and the adoption of the more global newspaper the *New York Times*. Always maintaining the focus on print media, Parra's photomontages work with the fragments of seductive advertising and captivating imagery recombined with the text of sensationalist news reporting and editorials to create new compositions. Similar to the Chilean narrators analyzed in chapter 2, Parra incorporates the language of monetarism (stocks, interest rates, debt, and credit) and advertising (the saturation and manipulation of the image) as a way of reflecting on the economization of life under neoliberalism.

How do avant-garde-inspired practices fare in regard to the neoliberal market strategies advanced after the coup? In other words, what is the relation between the economic "shock" policies of the period and the "shock" politics advanced by the Avanzada? As I argue in chapter 2, the neoliberal turn puts into question a utilitarian tradition of political economy associated with a critique of the bourgeois values of sobriety and asceticism. It demands a coming to terms with the economic values and practices of creative risk taking, flirting with the unpredictable, and gambling on novelty and difference. Novels such as Arturo Fontaine's *Oír su voz* give expression to this transition through entrepreneurial figures who formally reproduce the model of the avant-garde artist (with its imperative of innovation at any price) and neoliberal intellectuals (in the form of advertising executives) whose work consists in aestheticizing the visual culture of consumerism. So what is a critical visual art practice to do in circumstances when its antiinstitutional practices seem to have been effectively subsumed by the speculative logic of neoliberal capitalism?

The 1989 series *The Human Touch: The Final Edge* is representative of Parra's later work. In this series a full page Chemical Bank advertisement from the *New York Times* frames each individual piece. Parra maintains the header ("The Human Touch") and footer ("The Financial Edge") of the advertisement but empties it of its central image. In its place is a frame constituted by Susan B. Anthony one-dollar coins—stitched in place by Parra's signature red thread—that contains within it images such as a portrait fragment of a worried-looking Oliver North above a picture of conference chairs and a table from what appears to be the inside of a bank.[24] The dollar coins anachronistically frame the interior image fragments (which in this series include environmental issues, animal rights, political protests, the homeless, the military, etc.), intrinsically linking them to the world of corporate finance. The Susan B. Anthony coins serve as an anachronistic frame because they represent an attempt to reinstate a metallic currency in a world dominated by fiduciary forms of money.[25] In this way, the series marks the always shifting and aleatory forms of value associated with corporate finance. In this series the tension between text and image reveals the transition from the dictatorship-context *imbunche* (marked by censure and silence) to the neoliberal *imbunche*. With each corresponding piece in the *Human Touch* series, the imagery intrudes upon and begins to block the wording in the footer. Thus, "The Financial Edge" becomes "The Fin . . . al Edge" and ultimately just "The . . . Edge." If in the previously discussed 1977 piece *Diariamente* the interruption of the word *diariamente* by a tear containing blurred and barely recognizable people signified a concealed reference to the disappeared, then the transformation of the text "The Financial Edge" corresponds to a different logic. The challenge for the latter is no longer to find a code to communicate what in official spaces cannot be said, but rather to try and build alternative meanings by connecting and disconnecting the very material circulated by the information and advertising market. Nelly Richard describes Catalina Parra's visual arts project in the following way: "The work does not take refuge in the interiority of an 'I' in order to oppose itself to the world of capitalist visuality from the position of a language that is supposedly uncontaminated from its massificating procedures, but rather it constructs its oppositional signifieds from the same materiality that the visual rhetorics of the information and publicity market use in order to formulate their messages of dominance."[26] The difficulty here is that formulating the conflict in Parra's work as simply being an antagonism between "oppositional signifieds" and the market's "messages of dominance" doesn't account for the space of indeterminacy created by her work of connecting and disconnecting images and text. Through all the transformations that "The Financial Edge" undergoes in her series, it still stubbornly functions as both the frame and the support of the work. It is ultimately the archaic residues that Parra incorporates into her work that, more than any of the avant-garde strategies, interrupt the mass-media discourse of consumption and empty pluralism. It is the manual activity of sewing, as a vestigial practice remitting to an older cycle of accumulation, that signals the persistence of manual labor in the new global order. In the face of finance capital's evacuation of production sites (mines, factories, etc.) in favor of seeking maximization in nonproductive spaces like the stock market (where "money begets money"), Parra presents manual labor as the irreducible material stitching that holds together the cultures of abstraction.

This reveals a critical limitation in the way post-industrial and post-Fordist models of labor are conceptualized.[27] The overemphasis on the economic and cultural dominant ends up occluding the heterogeneity of emergent and residual forms. This strategy parallels the banking advertisement's desired effect of presenting a new global order that seamlessly couples together the human and the financial. The "human touch" and the "financial edge" are meant to combine together under the logic of human capital. Their distinctions collapse, and a logic emerges where life is measured as a strategy of self-appreciation or as an endless portfolio-building project. Gayatri Chakravorty Spivak's theorization of the economic text is a way of opening up these collapsed distinctions.

According to Spivak, Marx uncovers the economic text around 1857, when he investigates exploitation through a study of money. The economic text gives a textualized response to the question of value. It eschews essentialism and economic determinism. Marx's chain of value (Value→Money→Capital) is read as reversible, open-ended, and fraught with discontinuities. The assumption that value represents labor is critiqued because the value chain works not only through a representational logic but also through a differential one. Each dialectical step of the value chain leads into the "open-endedness of textuality," marked by indeterminacy, indifference, inadequacy, and rupture.[28] Spivak's focus on the economic text is part of a project that attempts to think the materialist predication of the subject. This is a definition of subjectivity made in materialist terms—that is, labor power—rather than idealist ones such as consciousness. For Spivak, the materialist predication of the subject is the subject defined by its capacity to produce more than itself. The emphasis on the materialist ground of the project is important because the textualization of the value chain (the economic text) is not meant to efface or disavow the economic question of exploitation. In other words, it is not a culturalist move. On the contrary, it is meant to maintain the visibility and centrality of labor, economics, and exploitation and the question of value in its materialist articulation, while at the same time abandoning earlier forms of economic determinism.

This move permits an understanding of the inequities of global exploitation that often gets left out of "radical critiques" of globalization and the discourse of marketing and business administration: "To state the problem in the philosophical idiom of this essay: as the subject as super-adequation in labor-power seems to negate itself within telecommunication, a negation of the negation is continually produced by the shifting lines of the international division of labor. This is why any critique of the labor theory of value, pointing at the unfeasibility of the theory under post-industrialism, or as a calculus of economic indicators, ignores the dark presence of the Third World."[29] The focus on the economic text makes visible the link between documents of civilization and documents of barbarism.[30] It reveals the anonymous toil of victims of the international division of labor, which, according to Spivak, in its most recent incarnation positions women as its surplus army of labor.[31] The double move of putting the economic text "under erasure," that is, revealing its textual indeterminacy and stripping it of all economism, while at the same time insisting on the pervasive and unavoidable quality of the economic question (the labor theory of value) brings into focus the complicity between cultural and economic value systems: "A 'culturalism' that disavows the economic in its global operations cannot get a grip on the concomitant production of barbarism."[32]

This returns us to the question with which we began this section, regarding the possibility of taking strategies that were developed in opposition to a repressive national security state (antidictatorial strategies) and deploying them in the face of an encroaching global market (the challenge of the neoliberal present). The error is to set this question up as a necessary taking of sides: Parra's dictatorship *imbunches* versus her neoliberal *imbunches.* Equally questionable is the gesture of falsely harmonizing what are, after all, irreconcilable differences. One of the important contributions that have emerged out of the work on transitions is the understanding that transitional moments are themselves always constituted by the tensions and struggles between coexisting modes of production. Thus Parra's visual arts practice cannot be reduced to either a refractory aesthetic that is inassimilable by the totalizing logic of the market or a foreclosed antiinstitutional avant-garde practice that has been effectively subsumed by the speculative logic of neoliberal capitalism. Rather—and this is the ultimate connection I want to establish between Donoso's literary project and Parra's visual arts project—much like Donoso's attempt at resuscitating a subversive and critical realism as a way of renewing an exhausted modernist aesthetic, Parra's deployment of what can be considered critically exhausted vanguard strategies (the thread-stitched photo-montages), in the context of reflecting on the market saturation and manipulation of the image, is in essence an attempt at resuscitating a critical avant-garde practice. Studying this tension in Parra between a critical visual-arts practice and a foreclosed or exhausted one doesn't give us a blueprint of what something resembling a contemporary avant-garde practice capable of critically reflecting on the economization of life under neoliberalism might actually look like, but it does present us with the opportunity and the obligation to theorize such a possibility.

5

REFLECTIONS ON A RESIDUAL FORMATION

Intellectual Work, Real Subsumption, and Socialized Labor

I begin with what may appear to be an unlikely starting point for a discussion of the relation between neoliberalism and the military coup: a debate over conflicting interpretations of Gabriela Mistral's poetry. The debate is one that transpired within the pages of the journal *Estudios Públicos* in 1985–86 and was ignited by a review that Patricio Marchant wrote about Jorge Guzman's book *Diferencias latinoamericanas.*[1] There is, I will argue, more at stake in this debate than just the status of literary criticism on Gabriela Mistral. It reveals differing perspectives regarding the legacies of the dictatorship and the state of intellectual discourse and critical thinking in dictatorial and postdictatorial Chile. In other words, if—as has been argued in the previous chapters—one of the effects of the neoliberal transition is the passage from the influence of the politician, the revolutionary, and the intellectual to the reign of the expert, the technician, and the technocrat, then what is the status of intellectual discourse in this transformed world?

Jorge Guzman's 1984 book of literary criticism, *Diferencias latinoamericanas,* engages in a careful reading of contemporary Latin American authors that attempts to bring to the fore the specifically regional nature of Latin American literature. In his chapter on Gabriela Mistral,

Guzman argues, for example, that her poetry can be characterized as a fatherless production. The father doesn't occupy the central place that supposedly maintains order and meaning in the Spanish language. In the father's place is an empty center. This absence, Guzman argues, marks Mistral's poetic discourse with an important distinction, a distinction that is then identified and explained as a specifically Latin American difference.

Although it is never explicitly addressed in any of the essays included in *Diferencias latinoamericanas* and only briefly mentioned in the "Nota previa," the book is strongly marked by the 1973 military coup. The intellectual project that informs Guzman's readings of Latin American literature is inextricably tied to the experience of the dictatorship. The date 11 September 1973 marks the beginning of what Guzman calls his *theoretical conversion,* a conversion catalyzed by disillusion and shock, where familiar literary works became strange and fascinating and where the problems with the application of metropolitan conceptual models to regional literature became visible, revealing, for example, how necessarily distorting it is to read César Vallejo as Jacques Derrida reads Stéphane Mallarmé: "In summary, it unhinges his relationship with his own world, which is equivalent to making him a stranger in his own world, it makes him a stranger to himself and makes him suspicious of the ideological, aesthetic, and epistemological tools that fabricated the illusion in which he lived. All of which make him realize that nothing is more important than studying the reality in which he has always lived." [2]

This revelation or theoretical conversion can be understood as a particular kind of nostalgia, one that is not reducible to the whimsical yearnings for the "good old days" nor easily characterized as the decadent, romantic, and ultimately conservative twin of memory (memory is almost always portrayed as affirmative and politically empowering in contrast to nostalgia). It is a nostalgia that refers back to the pathological roots of the concept: a disease caused by a separation from one's home or, in other words, homesickness. It is a homesickness where the longing for another time, another place, and another self reveals that we are all too comfortable, too at home, in our own time and in our own skin. Thus, in *Diferencias latinoamericanas* nostalgia appears as a potentially critical engagement with the present: an attempt to resuscitate critical thinking, which in this case takes the form of a regionalist critique of Latin American literary studies, after the catastrophe. The question is whether this regionalism that has been resuscitated as a way of confronting the present can shed its more reactive elements (such as its resistance to theory and its essentializing of the local) in order to critically think the present.

A parallel but markedly different articulation of the literary and the experience of dictatorship can be found in the work of the Chilean philosopher Patricio Marchant. Marchant's philosophic study of Chilean poetry is, like Guzman's *Diferencias latinoamericanas,* an example of an intellectual project marked by the dictatorship. In Marchant's case it is not the experience of dictatorship that makes possible new readings of literary texts; rather, it is the texts, in particular Gabriela Mistral's poetry, that make a profound understanding of the experience of dictatorship possible: "And of Chilean poetry, a discovery, in these years, of Mistralian poetry: it is as if this poetry needed the national catastrophe in order to begin to be understood. She, first and foremost, gives us the elements to begin this ineludible task: the commentary—in all the spaces of national life—of our catastrophe."[3] This necessary task of establishing the 1973 catastrophe as a catastrophe and not a temporary suspension of a democratic tradition implies for Marchant coming to terms with some of its consequences: the crisis of intellectual legitimacy, the fall into neoliberal technocracy, the triumph of instrumental reason, and the rise of the expert. For Marchant, the catastrophe renders impossible the modern intellectual's task of conceiving social life as a positive totality and also renders impossible the task of prescribing what is necessary to attain an emancipatory ideal (whether it be Christian, enlightenment, Marxist, liberal, etc.).

In order to establish a new reading of Mistral, Marchant breaks from prior scenes (what he refers to as the "sons of Mistral," among whom he includes Guzman). This implies breaking with transferential readings of Mistral that posit her as the "Madre por excelencia." Marchant avoids monumentalizing, and in the Deleuzian spirit of creating a "becoming-minor," he doesn't refer to a single poetic subject, but to readings of her multiplicity. Marchant describes this work as "writing about a poet, as if you were writing with the poet something else, which is the only way of reading her."[4] Reading Mistral as a poet who writes to the present and announces our actual desolation is possible for Marchant because of the dialogue he hears between Mistral's poetry (with its meditations on Latin America's indigenous people and mestizos and its meditations on desolation and defeat) and the problems facing contemporary philosophy. It is this relation that, in Marchant's eyes, makes Mistral's poetry essential for a thinking after the catastrophe, a rethinking of the role of the intellectual and a critical confrontation with the present. Marchant's reflections on the challenges of thinking the present and the place of the intellectual after the 1973 catastrophe return us to the problems touched upon in chapter 2, the neoliberal concept of labor, human capital, and the emerging articulations between intellectual work and conceptualizations of immaterial labor. In the following section I return to this problem but frame it from a different perspective: Marx's analysis of the real and the formal subsumption of labor under capital and his concept of socialized labor.

Real Subsumption, Socialized Labor, and Human Capital

Marx presents the formal subsumption of labor under capital as a transitional concept. Formal subsumption appears as always on its way to becoming real subsumption, and for that reason it has proven to be a powerful periodizing concept.[5] The transition from formal to real subsumption of labor has corollaries in Jameson's periodization of modernity and postmodernity and in Deleuze's work on disciplinary societies and societies of control; Hardt and Negri explicitly invoke the passage from formal to real subsumption when they discuss the transition from an imperialist phase of capitalism to what they call *empire*.

Marx conceives of formal subsumption of labor under capital as the imperialist and expansionist period of manufacture (for Marx this spans from the sixteenth century to the Industrial Revolution). Real subsumption of labor follows as the process of intensification and full interiorization of social relations to capital that Marx identified with the emergence of the modern factory.

Formal subsumption is expansionist in that it incorporates what is foreign to capital, more specifically preexisting labor processes. Thus—and these are two of the examples that Marx uses—under formal subsumption the feudal peasant becomes a day laborer, and the slave ceases to be an instrument of production, becoming a paid worker. In this way, archaic or preexisting labor processes are incorporated into capitalist labor, becoming instruments of valorization and the manufacturing of surplus value. Through formal subsumption, capitalism internalizes its outside. It is important to note that this process is understood as a simply *formal* change rather than a real one because the nature of the preexisting labor process is still recognizable as an archaic form even when it has been taken over by capital. For example, in the case of a peasant economy formally subsumed by capital, the activity that goes into making something like handicrafts remains essentially unchanged—the worker continues to basically do the same job. What changes is that there is a separation from the means of production (separation from the land), the peasant becomes a wage-laborer, his or her subsistence must be bought with the wage, surplus labor is extracted by extending the duration of labor-time (a lengthening of the work day), and in general work becomes more intensive and more continuous.

This is how Marx describes the process of formally subsuming preexisting labor processes to capital, or, in other words, capitalism's internalizing of its outside. Yet formally subsumed labor plus valorization is not what Marx conceives of as a *specifically* capitalist form of production (as we will see, that is where the real subsumption of labor comes in). Ultimately, the formal subsumption of labor under capital is limited to producing absolute surplus value—which is basically done by increasing the amount of labor-time—rather than producing relative surplus value, hence its status as a transitional process that is always on its way to becoming real subsumption, or capitalism proper. On the way it creates the conditions for real subsumption by developing the processes of secularization and rationalization and breaking up social and economic hierarchies. Wage labor introduces the values of versatility and adaptability and an indifference to the content of the work, and it strips social relations down to the purely economic.

Real subsumption of labor under capital is, for Marx, the coming into being of a *specifically* capitalist form of production. That is to say, with the production of relative surplus value, a labor process emerges that is born of capital and is intrinsic to it, rather than being an adaptation from something that comes from the outside (the latter corresponds to what Marx calls the formal subsumption of labor: the imperialist and expansionist period of manufacture that spans from the sixteenth century to the Industrial Revolution). In this sense, Marx's real subsumption of labor is referring to a complete revolution in the mode of production, in the productivity of the workers, and in the relations between workers and capitalists.[6] This capitalist revolution is characterized by the development of the social forces of production, the move to large-scale production, the direct application of science and technology, the creation of new demands and new needs, and the movement toward a fully realized world market.

In his brief discussion of real subsumption, Marx places particular emphasis on "socialized labor."[7] Under real subsumption, labor is not just about physical bodies being put to work in factories, but about capital becoming increasingly dependent on social knowledge, cooperation, and communication. Capital sheds any of the individual or private characteristics it may have had under formal subsumption and organizes its profit maximization around the collective team or the "cooperative totality." For Marx, socialized labor includes the engineers, the technologists, and the managers. It is part of the use of machinery and the harnessing of the sciences, mechanics, chemistry, and technology in order to surpass in both scale and intensity what is possible through individual labor. It is worth noting that the real subsumption of labor marks a limit in Marx's thinking, the limit of futurity: he gestures toward capitalism's increasing dependence on social knowledge, cooperation, and communication, which he sees as emerging in the context of the modern factory, but socialized labor doesn't fully come into its own until the move toward an information-based production of service, the move from, for example, Fordism to Toyotism, and the increasing focus on immaterial labor. It is in this context that Antonio Negri develops his take on the concept of the "socialized worker": the post-Fordist subject as heir to the revolutionary activity of the Fordist factory "mass worker." I want to take things in a different direction and connect socialized labor with the neoliberal labor theory of human capital.

What Marx was tentatively envisioning in the context of the real subsumption of labor under capital as socialized labor emerges in an intensified and radicalized form almost one hundred years later as the neoliberal concept of labor known as human capital. As we saw in chapter 2, Foucault defines American-style neoliberalism as the dual process of extending economic analyses into previously unexplored domains and applying an economic model to a sphere of human action previously thought to be noneconomic. The principal object of his study is neoliberalism's concept of labor: human capital. One of the things Foucault reveals is that American neoliberals have an unexpected point of contact with Karl Marx's reading of capital: they both identify the abstraction of labor as the principal problem with classical political economy. For Marx, capitalism transforms concrete labor into abstract labor power. The neoliberal perspective coincides with Marx in that the abstraction of labor is the problem, but rather than considering abstraction to be a product of capital accumulation, they consider labor abstraction to be a problem of how capitalism has been previously *theorized* by political economists. The neoliberal project purports to break with this tradition of abstracting labor by *reading* capitalist processes differently. Human capital is the result of this reading.

One of the questions raised by this alternative genealogy of Marx's socialized labor—alternative to the increasingly dominant framework of immaterial labor—is, what kind of leftist critique is adequate to the challenges of a labor model based on human capital? And is the model of immaterial labor up to that task, or is it a form of "new conformism" that gives a radical spin to the literature of business and official policy circles, as Keya Ganguly and others have suggested?[8] One important step that a focus on the logic of human capital permits us to take is to move beyond a humanist critique of neoliberalism that retrenches in the position that human qualities such as desires and subjectivities cannot be reduced to the logics of supply and demand and that they exist beyond the logic of the commodity form.

The Chilean philosopher Willy Thayer's essay "Fin del 'trabajo intelectual' y fin idealista/capitalista de la historia en la 'era de la subsunción real del capital'" [The end of "intellectual labor" and the idealist/capitalist end of history in the "age of the real subsumption of capital"] offers an original take on the problem of real subsumption, which is firmly situated in the tradition of reading "Marx beyond Marx." Focusing on the emergence and increasing importance of socialized labor in Marx's conceptualization of real subsumption, Thayer advances the provocative claim that the abolition of the difference between intellectual and physical labor that is purportedly brought about under the real subsumption of labor under capital signals the end of the social division of labor in general. Perversely then, the end of the social division of labor, which has traditionally been linked to the end of the state, the end of class struggle, and the arrival of communism, is not brought into being by the revolution, but rather by the intensification (the real subsumption) of the capitalist process.

For Thayer, one of the far-reaching consequences that this obliteration of the difference between physical and intellectual labor has is that it produces a chain reaction blurring the differences between action and meaning, exteriority and interiority, and nature and history. The indifferent absorption of physical and intellectual labor into the process of valorization, represented in the figure of socialized labor, puts into question the very possibility of genuinely critical practice. If there is no difference between action and meaning, then there is no place for a critical faculty that questions the meaning of action. For Thayer, real subsumption's combination of socialized labor and valorization annuls the question regarding the meaning of action. What Thayer is referring to here in regard to socialized labor is similar to what Bourdieu and Wacquant identify as the two new types of cultural producers who have taken the place of the traditional intellectual in the transition from the state to the market: the expert who prepares highly technical documents to justify policy made on non-technical grounds and the "communication consultant to the prince" who gives an academic veneer to the political projects of the neoliberal state and the business nobility.[9]

Thayer leaves us with the following dilemma: the difference between Sisyphus and the contemporary intellectual is that not only is Sisyphus condemned to the physical labor of ceaselessly pushing a rock up a hill, but he is at the same time condemned to the intellectual labor of realizing the meaninglessness of his actions. The intellectual in the age of the real subsumption of labor under capital has the "advantage" of dissolving this conflict by disappearing into the category of socialized labor. This "advantage" comes at the expense of no longer making a claim to a critical faculty.

These problems are productively taken up in the 2005 novel *En la sombra del dinero,* by the Chilean writer Ramón Díaz Eterovic. *En la sombra del dinero* promises a combination of the timeliest of subject matters: an analysis of the money form in contemporary Chile with a genre that has functioned as a critique of the dictatorship and post-dictatorship period: the hard-boiled detective novel. Surprisingly, the result turns out to be an exercise in anachronism. The space of money that the novel focuses on, the corrupt Servicio de Inversiones Públicas, is a state-run institution that has been all but abandoned in the context of the neoliberal economic transformations that Chile has experienced since the 1970s (deregulation, privatization, withdrawal of the state from areas of social provision, etc.). The Servicio de Inversiones Públicas appears in the novel as a museum piece, a semi-abandoned relic of a national popular past. In its interior, the reader is introduced to a group of ghostly figures: public employees living empty, pointless lives, bemoaning their broken dreams. These appear as truly Sisyphus-like figures whose torment lies less in the futility and monotony of their work than in the acute awareness that this is the condition of their existence.

The crime and outcome of the novel are simple and conventional enough: a public employee discovers that funds are being siphoned off to pay for a senator's electoral campaign. Being a member of the political party in question, the public employee remains silent. When he discovers that the money is being pocketed, he threatens to reveal everything and is murdered. At this level there is something profoundly disappointing about this novel: the reader is left with the sense that the genre that has opened up an important avenue for critique seems to have been reduced to simply articulating a moralistic condemnation of corruption. In the novel everyone knows that what is ultimately behind the mystery is money, but it is constantly suggested that there is more to it. One way of understanding the return to the seemingly anachronistic space of the state institution is that, as the title suggests, the novel really does occur in the shadow of money, because the real machinations of power remain allusively elsewhere.

The seemingly anachronistic return to the site of the state institution performs something that, at first glance, seems to be a paradoxical operation: a return to the logic of formal subsumption in the era of real subsumption; it is a return to the process of privatization of what was exterior to capitalism (understood here as a particular way of extracting surplus value: relative as opposed to absolute). What is uncanny about this return is that it is enacted from a moment when there no longer seems be an outside to internalize, when privatization seems to have run its course. Perhaps what *En la sombra del dinero*'s anachronistic return to the site of formal subsumption is gesturing toward is a way to begin to imagine what a materialist practice might look like in the era of real subsumption: a permanent guerrilla attack against the logic of dedifferentiation, against the collapsing of the difference between physical and intellectual labor and the difference between action and meaning. Marx's emphasis on the socialization of labor in relation to real subsumption has been developed in different directions. A neo-Spinozian take on it emphasizes the utopic potential that could be unleashed by this cooperative totality. Thayer, on the other hand, sees it as the demise of any critical intellectual practice (Sisyphus is freed by no longer being able to reflect on the futility of his task). Both positions are premised on the idea that formal subsumption is an "early stage" of capitalism on its way to becoming real subsumption. What is needed is a more differential articulation of the relation between formal and real subsumption that can take into account the multiple modes of surplus-value extraction that are hierarchically present in any given historical period.

Reflections on a Residual Formation

The task of this study has been to explore the inner solidarity between different transitional forms: the economic (the neoliberal transition from the state to the market), the political (the transition from dictatorship to democracy), and the aesthetic (here I've focused on the literary transition from modernist boom novels to emerging forms of neorealist fiction; the transition in Patricio Guzmán's documentary project from memory politics to a reflection on the problems of restitution; and the transition from a refractory visual-arts practice to one that explores and incorporates the market problems of debt, consumption, and the saturation of the image). Taking a long historical view of the origins of Chile's capitalist transformation and its adoption of the neoliberal economic model, I have found in a number of literary and visual texts that are working through the implications of these transitions the emergence of speculative cultural forms such as antiallegorical strategies, second-order forms of abstraction, the dissemination of a stock-market model of value, and avant-garde models of political economy.

The different literary and visual texts that have been included in this study do not purport to offer a representative sampling of postdictatorship fiction—this study has no pretences of being a literary history; rather, the selections represent critical scenes where still-emergent and precarious insights are being articulated around the central question concerning the relation between culture and the market in the context of the Chilean neoliberal transition. These insights begin with Donoso's rethinking of the tension between realist and modernist representation in light of the crisis of the gold standard and the dominance of dematerialized currencies. It is this focus on dematerialization that leads a novel like *Casa de campo,* which is itself an allegorization of the 1973 military coup, to explore antiallegorical practices and the emergence of new forms of abstraction. The latter, I've argued, are harbingers of the sea change that the speculative logic of neoliberal capitalism will introduce during the dictatorship period. This passage that Donoso's novel signals, from allegorical abstraction to commodity abstraction, is then intensified and further explored by future generations of writers and artists. Such is the case with Arturo Fontaine's political economization of the novel form in *Oír su voz.* I have argued that a similar project, with vastly different political and critical implications, can be found in the shift that *Mano de obra* represents in relation to Eltit's prior literary project. This is a shift from a refractory or melancholic aesthetics to one that takes on the task of narrating emerging neoliberal forms (it is a novel where the nonplace of the supermarket stands in for the territorialized moment of past industrial production, and the so-called post-Fordist notion of servile virtuosity stands in for the collective labor movements of the past).

What then are speculative fictions? In the texts I have been working with, the idea of speculative fiction corresponds to the different forms of speculative abstraction associated with finance capitalism that can be understood as an intensification and overcoming of allegorical abstraction. In the case of the Chilean neoliberal transition, I have periodized this process beginning with Donoso's failed neorealist project and the challenge he lays down for future generations of writers and artists to think through the implications of these emerging speculative cultural forms. First, my readings of speculative fictions seek to move beyond any kind of aesthetic retrenchment as a possible response to the problems of the market in contemporary society. The market, it should be noted, is understood here in a very specific, very neoliberal, way: it denotes a rationality that not only seeks to govern society in the name of the economy but that redefines the social sphere as a wholly economic domain. Thinking the relation between culture and the market in this light demands the inclusion of economic and market analysis alongside textual analysis.

More challenging than the limitations of aesthetic retrenchment is the culturalist pitfall of demanding that culture do the work previously accorded to the economical and political spheres. This substitutional logic (substituting culture for either politics or economics) risks the promotion of ultimately unsatisfactory cultural "fixes" to deeply rooted social problems. This is, for example, what is at stake in chapter 3, where I critique *Fernando ha vuelto*'s cultural discourse of closure, which is premised on the allegorized figure of forensics as a fully restitutional project. In its place I offer a reading of this documentary (along with Guzmán's documentary project) along the lines of a restitutional project that opens up the possibility of questioning the kinds of scales and systems of equivalencies or exchange that are drawn upon to account for historical wrongs that lie beyond measure.

NOTES

Introduction

1. "Tu deber es estudiar lo que es grande en tu patria, la poesía chilena": Patricio Marchant, *Sobre arboles y madres* (Santiago: Ediciones Gato Murr, 1984), 27. Unless otherwise noted, all translations from the Spanish are my own.

2. The focus on the concept of a transition builds on a rich literature in Latin American cultural theory that includes thinkers such as Willy Thayer, Tomás Moulian, Federico Galende, Sergio Villalobos, Alberto Moreiras, Nelly Richard, Brett Levinson, Francine Masiello, Gareth Williams, and Idelber Avelar.

3. This understanding of finance capital as a cyclical and transitional moment in the history of capital accumulation is based on Giovanni Arrighi's model, laid out in *The Long Twentieth Century: Money, Power, and the Origins of Our Times* (London: Verso, 1999).

4. Tomás Moulian, *Chile actual: Anatomía de un mito* (Santiago: LOM, 1997), 88.

5. Chapter 1 develops this argument in greater depth and detail.

6. I am referring to markers such as the consequences the 2002 economic meltdown in Argentina had for the region, the so-called left turns in Latin America, and the resurgence of neo-Keynesian ideas during the current global economic crisis. One of the strongest articulations of this position can be found in Fernando Leiva's work on post-neoliberal development.

7. Popular Unity (Unidad Popular) refers to the alliance of left-wing political parties formed in Oct. 1969. It included the Socialist Party, the Communist

Party, the Radical Party, the Movimiento de Acción Popular Unitario (MAPU), the Partido Social Demócrata (PSD), and the Acción Popular Independiente (API). It was led by Salvador Allende and governed Chile for one thousand days between 1970 and the 1973 military coup.

8. This period is characterized by the adoption of the import-substitution industrialization model, urbanization, massive unionizing campaigns (most notably of rural workers between 1965 and 1970), the reform of the electoral system (to include woman's and illiterate suffrage), state-managed social security, education, a public health system, and mass media (e.g., monopolized television). The exhaustion or deterioration of this order is then characterized by political polarization, a growing antagonism between workers and capitalists, an economy that cannot keep up with chronic inflation, and the failure of the political class to administer the consequences of a modernization process they initiated—that is to say, the institutional canalization of the "rebelión de las masas" (the result being strikes and protests). Popular Unity emerges in this moment of conflict proposing nationalization (principally copper), expropriation (agrarian reform), and the redistribution of wealth.

9. Javier Martínez and Arturo Díaz, *Chile: The Great Transformation* (Washington, DC: Brookings Institute, 1996), 48.

10. See Carlos Huneeus, *The Pinochet Regime* (Boulder: Lynne Rienner Publishers, 2007).

11. When considering the main legacies of the administrations preceding the 1973 military coup—specifically the Christian Democrat "revolution within freedom" period (1964–70) and the Popular Unity period (1970–73)—what is frequently highlighted is the nationalization of copper, agrarian reform, literacy campaigns, and university reform. It is worth reflecting on the first two because, perhaps counterintuitively, they reveal an important continuity between periods that have been traditionally understood as ruptured: the Frei Montalva/Allende period and the Pinochet and Concertación period. The fact that Pinochet maintained state ownership of CODELCO (the national mining company formed during the Popular Unity period) cannot simply be written off as one exception to the massive privatization of state services that characterized this period. Copper mining was and continues to be the single most important and profitable economic industry in Chile. It has been argued that state ownership of CODELCO was one of the reasons the other privatizations were possible: it financed an important part of the Chilean state's budget and provided the state with the necessary autonomy to implement the reforms. The point is that the origins of Chile's capitalist revolution predate the dictatorship, and the modernizing work done beforehand needs to be taken into account.

The case of agrarian reform makes an even stronger argument for this position. The reform (initiated during the Frei Montalva government in 1967) definitively ended with the *inquilinaje* or *latifundio* system and radically altered the Chilean landscape (it affected practically all cultivated lands). After the military coup, with the exception of a limited number of cases, the expropriated lands were not returned to the previous owners. Part of the land, the reserve, was left to the old proprietors; a majority of it was delivered to the peasants; and part was auctioned off to large forestry companies and medium-sized modern agribusinesses. Besides a decline in the number of people employed in agriculture and a sharp climb in urbanization, the most profound effect of this was the creation of a market in land that exploded the static agricultural structure based around the latifundio system. Thus, the transition was accelerated by agrarian reform. Its modernizing potential was then appropriated and recanalized by the dictatorship. Martínez and Díaz have pushed this argument the furthest. They argue that the decade of progressive reforms (1964–73) and the seventeen years of neoliberal reforms (1973–90) were led not by markets or civil society, but rather by the state and by elites firmly rooted in it. Although the 1964–73 reforms had a totally different orientation from the neoliberal reforms, there is an important continuity between the two periods.

12. This literature reveals that the actual process was not as neat and free of contradictions and internal inconsistencies as the division into distinct stages may imply. There were different civilian and military forces competing to impose a new post–Popular Unity project of Chilean modernity. For an analysis of the internal conflicts that the implementation of the neoliberal project had within the military (specifically the conflicts between statist and nonstatist positions) see Veronica Valdivia's "Estatismo y neoliberalismo: un contrapunto militar. Chile 1973–1979," *Historia* 34 (2001): 167–226.

13. I do not include the period between 1973 and 1975 because these years were more about attempting to normalize the economic situation after the military coup than initiating structural change. It was also not immediately clear what economic direction the country would move in. Within the armed forces there were conflicting positions. as revealed by the debate between air force general Gustavo Leigh, who was a follower of the ideas of Keynes and defended a strong and central role for the state, and Augusto Pinochet, who would go on to appoint "Chicago Boys" to key economic posts.

14. In what is to this day the most thorough study of the connection between the Chicago School of Economics and the Chilean neoliberal experiment, Juan Gabriel Valdés proposes that it was a strictly unilateral relationship: it was in his words "a deliberate process of transferring ideas from one coun-

try to another" (xi). As a part of the Cold War program against left-wing tendencies in Latin America, the United States had been funding the training of Chilean economists in Chicago since as early as the 1950s. The result was that Chicago-trained economists dominated the Universidad Católica, and groups like "The Monday Club" (an organization of business elites who organized against Popular Unity) funded the work of neoliberal economists through research institutes and think tanks. So even before the 1973 military coup the ground had already been prepared for the implementation of the economic experiment. See Juan Gabriel Valdés, *Pinochet's Economists: The Chicago School in Chile* (Cambridge: Cambridge University Press, 1995).

15. See Huneeus, *Pinochet Regime;* Valdivia, "Estatismo y neoliberalismo"; and Valdés, *Pinochet's Economists.*

16. Peter Winn, ed., *Victims of the Chilean Miracle: Workers and Neoliberalism in the Pinochet Era, 1973–2002* (Durham: Duke University Press, 2004), 34.

17. These are texts written both from the right and from the left, which include among others David Harvey's *A Brief History of Neoliberalism* (Oxford: Oxford University Press, 2007); Niall Ferguson's *The Ascent of Money* (New York: Penguin Press, 2008); and Naomi Klein's *The Shock Doctrine* (New York: Metropolitan Books, 2007).

18. Brett Levinson, *Market and Thought: Meditations on the Political and the Biopolitical* (New York: Fordham University Press, 2004), 1.

19. Georg Simmel, *The Philosophy of Money* (London: Routledge, 1978), 54.

20. Fredric Jameson, "Globalization and Political Strategy," *New Left Review* 4 (July–Aug. 2000): 53.

21. Michel Foucault, *The Birth of Biopolitics: Lectures at the Collège de France 1978–1979,* ed. Michel Senellart (New York: Palgrave Macmillan, 2008), 79.

22. Karl Polanyi, *The Great Transformation* (Boston: Beacon Press, 1954), 256.

23. Manuel Antonio Garretón, *Hacia una nueva era política: estudio sobre las democratizaciones* (Mexico: Fondo de Cultura Económica, 1995), 15.

24. Winn, *Victims of the Chilean Miracle,* 3.

Chapter 1. The Brooder's Startled Gaze

1. Quoted in Carlos Cerda, *José Donoso: Originales y metáforas* (Santiago: Planeta, 1988), 68.

2. José Donoso, *Casa de campo,* 4th ed. (Barcelona: Editorial Seix Barral, 1981), 53: "lo hago con el modesto fin de proponer al público que acepte lo que escribo como un artificio."

3. Donoso, *Casa de campo,* 53.

4. See, e.g., Antonio Skármeta's 1975 critique of the boom writers for their refusal to accept the conventional face of reality, their avoidance of plot-centered novels, their avoidance of overt political commitment, their lack of proletarian characters and settings, and their overreliance on technical virtuosity: "Perspectiva de los novísmimos." *Hispamérica* 28 (1981): 49–65.

5. The debate I am referring to is not a single coherent text, but a wide constellation spanning different periods and literary traditions in the Global North and South. For the purposes of this essay the most relevant exchanges include: Ernest Bloch and Georg Lukács, in Theodor Adorno et al., *Aesthetics and Politics* (London: Verso, 1977), 16–59; Bertolt Brecht and Lukács, in Adorno et al. *Aesthetics and Politics,* 68–85; José María Arguedas and Julio Cortázar, in José María Arguedas, *El zorro de arriba y el zorro de abajo* (Paris: ALLCA XX, 1996), 7–22; Perry Anderson and Marshal Berman, in Perry Anderson, "Marshall Berman: Modernity and Revolution," in Anderson, *A Zone of Engagement* (London: Verso, 1992), 25–55; and Antonio Cornejo Polar and José Donoso, in Cornejo Polar, "José Donoso y los problemas de la nueva narrativa hispanoamericana," in *José Donoso: la destrucción de un mundo,* ed. Antonio Cornejo Polar (Buenos Aires: Editorial Fernando García Cambeiro, 1975), 109–22.

6. David Harvey, *The Condition of Postmodernity: An Enquiry into the Origins of Cultural Change* (Cambridge: Blackwell, 1990), 261.

7. Harvey, *Condition of Postmodernity,* 265.

8. Fredric Jameson, "Culture and Finance Capital," in *The Cultural Turn: Selected Writings on the Postmodern, 1983–1998* (London: Verso, 1998), 139.

9. Anderson, "Marshall Berman," 40.

10. Anderson, "Marshall Berman," 40

11. Cornejo Polar, "José Donoso," 111: "Sea porque nada cambia, sea porque todo vuelve a repetirse, una vez más, girando en un círculo inacabable, la historia deviene imposible."

12. Cornejo Polar, "José Donoso," 111: "es un cruel simulacro que parece crear cuando en verdad destruye."

13. This is a fundamental distinction for Cornejo Polar's project, and it is a response to the critiques directed toward Cornejo Polar's concept of heterogeneity that claim that it is epistemologically invalid because it is too general and can be applied to almost any literary tradition anywhere in the world. The argument goes: if it can be shown that ultimately all literatures are heterogeneous, then what is the specificity of *indigenismo*'s heterogeneity and, by extension, Latin American literary heterogeneity? See, e.g., Roberto Paoli's critique "Sobre el concepto de heterogeneidad: a proposito del indigenismo literario," *Revista de crítica literaria latinoamericana* 6, no. 12 (1980): 257–63,

and Cornejo Polar's response, which emphasizes the need to historicize every instance of cultural heterogeneity: "Respuesta a Roberto Paoli," *Revista de crítica literaria latinoamericana* 6, no. 12 (1980): 264–67.

14. Antonio Cornejo Polar, "El indigenismo y las literaturas heterogéneas," in *Sobre Literatura y Crítica Latinoamericanas* (Caracas: Ediciones de la facultad de humanidades y educación Universidad Central de Venezuela, 1982), 73: "una sociedad que habla a sí misma."

15. See Georg Lukács, "The Ideology of Modernism," in *Realism in Our Time: Literature and the Class Struggle,* trans. John Mander and Necke Mander (New York: Merlin Press, 1962), 597–611.

16. For a nuanced reading of La Manuela see Severo Sarduy's essay "Escritura/Travestismo," in *Escrito sobre un cuerpo* (Buenos Aires: Editorial Sudamericana, 1969), which focuses on the centrality of *travestismo* and inversion in *El lugar sin límites*.

17. Donoso, *Casa de campo,* 492.

18. Karl Marx, *Capital: A Critique of Political Economy,* vol. 1, trans. Ben Fowkes (London: Penguin Books, 1990), 873.

19. Louis Althusser and Étienne Balibar, *Reading Capital*, trans. Ben Brewster (London: Verso, 1999), 276.

20. Donoso, *Casa de campo,* 174: "para estos dos seres la fiesta no existía, que su búsqueda no modificaba su comportamiento, que eran secos, pura estructura, puro designio."

21. Donoso, *Casa de campo,* 204: "sólo se proponía desarticular, desmontar el mundo de su padre, para que así su odio quedara desprovisto de objeto, y ser inefectivo, no la hiriera."

22. Donoso, *Casa de campo,* 191: "que sabía con exactitud las cantidades, pesos, valor, producción y disponibilidad del metal que enriquecía a la familia."

23. Donoso, *Casa de campo,* 192: "no se conformaba con que intentara covencerla que el oro era sólo una idea existente en libros de cuenta y transacciones, que sólo vendido, comerciado, exportado, ahorrado, transformado en bonos y acciones, en préstamos e hipotecas, adquiría valor, y no lo poseía, en cambio, en sí mismo, como sustancia sacrosanta que a ella no se le permitía ver."

24. Marx, *Capital,* 227.

25. Randall Hinshaw, *Monetary Reform and the Price of Gold: Alternative Approaches* (Baltimore: Johns Hopkins University Press, 1967), 51.

26. Milton Friedman, *The Essence of Friedman* (Palo Alto: Hoover Institution Press, 1987), 379.

27. For a study of the connection between the crisis of literary realism and the end of gold money in the nineteenth century, see Goux's *The Coiners of Language,* trans. Jennifer Curtiss Gage (Norman: University of Oklahoma Press, 1994).

28. Donoso, *Casa de campo,* 177: "Escarbó en el oro pulverizado que tiñó sus brazos como sangre amarilla, sus manos, sus coyunturas, las uñas relucientes. La cara metalica, el pelo como una espuma de oro. Volaban las partículas de metal molido por sus manos sanguinarias, las pestañas de oro, las cejas de oro, la mueca de su sonrisa infantil transformada en una máscara eterna de encono."

29. Donoso, *Casa de campo,* 421: "lo que ellos *eran* carecía de todo valor para los extranjeros."

30. Donoso, *Casa de campo,* 448: "El subjetivismo con que ustedes acostumbran a juzgar todo lo que pertence a la familia nada tiene que ver con la realidad vista desde afuera y con otra perspectiva."

31. The best-known texts regarding this discussion include Walter Benjamin's *The Origin of German Tragic Drama* (London: Verso, 1998) and Paul de Man's "The Rhetoric of Temporality," in *Blindness and Insight: Essays in the Rhetoric of Contemporary Criticism,* 2nd ed. (Minneapolis: University of Minnesota Press, 1983), 187–228.

32. Hans Georg Gadamer, *Truth and Method* (New York: Continuum, 2004), 63.

33. Ignacio Valente, "José Donoso: *Casa de Campo,*" *El Mercurio* [Santiago], 3 May 1979. "Ignacio Valente" is the pseudonym used by the Opus Dei priest, poet, and influential literary critic José Miguel Ibáñez Langlois, who published in the pages of the newspaper *El Mercurio* during the dictatorship. He has been famously satirized in Roberto Bolaño's novel *By Night in Chile.*

34. Fredric Jameson, "From Metaphor to Allegory," in *Anything,* ed. Cynthia C. Davidson (New York: MIT Press, 2001), 27.

35. Idelber Avelar, *The Untimely Present* (Durham: Duke University Press, 1999), 232.

36. Walter Benjamin, *The Arcades Project,* trans. Howard Eiland and Kevin McLaughlin (Cambridge: Harvard University Press, 2002), 22.

37. Richard Halpern, *Shakespeare among the Moderns* (Ithaca: Cornell University Press, 1997), 27.

38. Donoso, *Casa de campo,* 117: "efectos implacablemente definidos."

39. Donoso, *Casa de campo,* 78: "la liberación era solo intelectual, teórica, pero bastaba; o bastaría cuando se completara."

40. Georg Lukács, "On Walter Benjamin," *New Left Review* 110 (1978): 84.

Chapter 2. Literature and Labor

1. The film fictionalizes one of Popular Unity's social-integration experiments, carried out at the Colegio Saint George. The rector of the school during this period was Father Gerardo Whelan, to whose memory the film is dedicated.

2. *Machuca,* dir. Andrés Woods, 121 min., DVD (Tornasel Films, 2004): "¡No, no, no! ¡No tengo nada que ver! ¡No soy de aquí! ¡No tengo nada que ver! ¡Soy del otro lado del río! ¡Mirame!"

3. Moulian, *Chile actual,* 88: "es la puerta de entrada al paraíso del consumo a través del purgatorio del endeudamiento."

4. Moulian, *Chile actual,* 107: "Es el purgatorio de la explotación acrecentada, junto con el cielo de la amplificación de las posibilidades consumatorias."

5. Néstor García Canclini, *Consumers and Citizens: Globalization and Multicultural Conflicts,* trans. George Yúdice (Minneapolis: University of Minnesota Press, 2001), 5.

6. Canclini, *Consumers and Citizens,* 18.

7. Canclini, *Consumers and Citizens,* 106; Diamela Eltit, *El padre mío* (Santiago: Francisco Zegers Editor, 1989), 17: "Jirones de diarios, fragmentos de exterminio, sílabas de muerte, pausas de mentira, frases comerciales, nombres de difuntos. Es una honda crisis del lenguaje, una infección en la memoria, una desarticulación de todas las ideologías. Es una pena, pensé. Es Chile, pensé."

8. Canclini, *Consumers and Citizens,* 13.

9. Armando Uribe, *Primera Linea,* 2002, http://www.primeralinea.cl/p4_plinea/site/20020818/pags/19800102122312.html:

> En ese momento [Fontaine] estaba escribiendo *Oír su voz* y me relató de que se trataba esta novela, que me pareció de sumo interés porque contenía una gran cantidad de hechos de orden económico financiero y político. Cuando la terminó se la pasó a su director de taller que había sido Donoso. Y Donoso le dijo que cómo era posible que metiera estos asuntos de las mesas de dinero y todo lo relacionado al período de las grandes quiebras de comienzos de los ochenta, cuando eso nadie lo entendía y a nadie le interesaba, en circunstancias que había sido un hecho colectivo chileno muy importante. Donoso le había dicho que tenía que meter un adulterio porque eso si que interesaba, y efectivamente la parte más débil de la novela es la del adulterio. Eso le demuestra un caso de desconexión con la realidad.

10. Following a similar line of investigation, Luis E. Cárcamo-Huechante's book *Tramas del mercado: imaginación economica, cultura pública y literatura en el Chile de fines del siglo veinte* (Santiago: Editorial Cuarto Propio, 2007), ex-

plores the relations among economics, politics, and Alberto Fuguet's narrative production.

11. See the Centro de Estudios Públicos's Web site: http://www.cepchile.cl.

12. Arturo Fontaine Talavera, "Trends toward Globalization in Chile," in *Many Globalizations: Cultural Diversity in the Contemporary World,* ed. Peter L. Berger and Samuel Huntington (Oxford: Oxford University Press, 2002), 251.

13. Talavera, "Trends toward Globalization in Chile," 252.

14. Ignacio Valente, "Una larga novela frustrada," *El Mercurio* [Santiago], 30 July 1992.

15. Neil Larsen, *Determinations: Essays on Theory, Narrative and Nation in the Americas* (London: Verso, 2001), 147.

16. The term "Chicago boys" refers to the approximately one hundred Chilean economy students trained at the University of Chicago through an agreement made possible by the Universidad Católica between the years 1957 and 1970. Juan Gabriel Valdés's *Pinochet's Economists* is the most thorough study of this group.

17. Arturo Fontaine Talavera, *Oír su voz* (Santiago: Planeta, 1992), 99: "el empresario latinoamericano de viejo cuño."

18. Talavera, *Oír su voz,* 99: "sin principios, inescrupuloso, oportunista, con una fortuna familiar construida al amporo de franquicias gubernamentales oligopólicas, y conservada a punta de astucia, avaricia, retiros de utilidades para hacer depósitos en el extranjero y falta de imaginación."

19. Talavera, *Oír su voz,* 189: "Un negocio no requiere capital, ni nada. Todo puede comprarse o arrendarse. Para eso está el mercado. Lo que vale es el concepto. Y el concepto es siempre una anticipación. . . . Por eso vivimos colgando del futuro que inventamos. Nuestra riqueza de hoy brota de lo que aún no existe, del mañana, quiero decir, de lo que valdrá mañana."

20. Talavera, *Oír su voz,* 112: "el poder del Estado sobre el valor del bien más comerciable de todos, el dinero"; "las dos caras del poder, de La Moneda: el monopolio de la violencia y el de la fabricación del dinero."

21. This list represents a group of Keynesian, "Cambridge School," and heterodox Marxian economists.

22. Talavera, *Oír su voz,* 49: "se convirtió así en el inspirador y encubierto cirujano de una vasta y compleja operación de ingeniería social."

23. Michel Foucault, *The History of Sexuality, Vol. 1* (New York: Vintage, 1990).

24. Talavera, *Oír su voz,* 50: "implantar esta nueva lengua oficial, un equivalente del sánscrito en la antigua India o del francés en el San Petersburgo decimonónico."

25. Talavera, *Oír su voz,* 51: "Y él tenía la certidumbre científica de conocer el remedio: era una preparación inyectable. Penosa, pero efectiva. Los militares le permitían colocarla. No le arredraba el cálculo de ese dolor."

26. Talavera, *Oír su voz,* 37: "Prefería mantenerse a distancia y no dejarse embrollar por la corporeidad de esos procesos productivos que, en la mente del financista, son únicamente otro tipo de pagarés. Le gustaba que el objeto de su pasión tomara formas abstractas."

27. Talavera, *Oír su voz,* 28: "una espesura verde y frondosa como una selva. 'Un filón de oro,' pensó, 'de oro vegetal.'"

28. Talavera, *Oír su voz,* 22: "Porque el dinero tenía la virtud de transmutar la vida de una persona y darle ese halo misterioso e irresistible, ese reconocimiento, esa impresión de logro y solidez que nada ni nadie podían desmentir."

29. Talavera, *Oír su voz,* 22: "La plata siempre es . . . la plata. Cuando todo falla, a la hora de los quiubo, sólo Don Dinero sigue siendo Don Dinero."

30. Foucault, *History of Sexuality, Vol. 1,* 30. For the most part Foucault bases his discussion of American neoliberalism on the published writings of Gary S. Becker and Theodor W. Schultz.

31. This corresponds to a labor theory of value, where value is ultimately determined by the variable of time; the work of David Ricardo is perhaps the best example. See his *Principles of Political Economy and Taxation* (New York: Prometheus Books, 1996).

32. Foucault, *Birth of Biopolitics,* 218.

33. Foucault, *Birth of Biopolitics,* 223.

34. Foucault, *Birth of Biopolitics,* 226.

35. Valdés, *Pinochet's Economists,* 252.

36. Schwartz is referring to the contradictions that emerge in nineteenth-century Brazil when liberal ideas are based on a slave economy. Here the parallel is with free-market ideas based on an authoritarian regime.

37. Quoted in Valdés, *Pinochet's Economists,* 30.

38. According to *El ladrillo,* the specific steps needed for the accumulation of human capital in the Chilean case include: the decentralization and privatization of schools, universities, hospitals, and other state-run institutions; an increase in technical training for teachers and other workers; the specialization of manual labor; and the replacement of shanty towns with private low-cost housing.

39. For a discussion of these differences see Martin Hopenhayn's "¿Qué tienen contra los sociólogos?" in *Arte en Chile desde 1973. Escena de avanzada y sociedad,* coord. Nelly Richard (Santiago: FLACSO, 1986), 93–100.

40. Nelly Richard, "The Reconfiguration of Post-Dictatorship Critical Thinking," *Journal of Latin American Cultural Studies* 3 (2000): 15.

41. Walter Benjamin, "The Work of Art in the Age of Mechanical Reproduction," in *Illuminations,* ed. Hannah Arendt, trans. Harry Zohn (New York: Schocken Books, 1969), 218.

42. Paolo Virno, "Virtuosity and Revolution: The Political Theory of Exodus," in *Radical Thought in Italy: A Potential Politics,* ed. Paolo Virno and Michael Hardt (Minneapolis: University of Minnesota Press, 1996), 201.

43. Diamela Eltit, *Mano de obra* (Santiago: Seix Barral, 2002), 22: "un extenso servilismo laboral."

44. Eltit, *Mano de obra,* 18: "se va a pique mi existencia."

45. Eltit, *Mano de obra,* 18: "en esos momentos, cuando ya se ha desencadenado un clímax de pacotilla, mi vida carece totalmente de sentido."

46. Eltit, *Mano de obra,* 23: "La terrible palabra destructiva que me dirigen, retumba en mi cabeza y me hace sentir mal. Me hiere y me perfora la palabra abriendo un boquete en mi riñon. Mehiere. Me perfora. Me impulsa a pensar que el trabajo, la que le dedico toda mi energía, no vale la pena."

47. Eltit, *Mano de obra,* 23: "Es posible que no merezca que los clientes me traten tan mal."

48. Eltit, *Mano de obra,* 17: "Me muerdo la lengua. La controlo, la castigo hasta el límite de la herida. Muerdo el dolor. Y ordeno el ojo."

49. Eltit, *Mano de obra,* 35: "Un goce que puedo comprender muy bien porque soy parte de ese deseo, de su necesidad de dejarme expuesto a la cámara, para así enteramente vengativo, duplicar después su éxtasis, en parte universal, con el producto."

50. Eltit, *Mano de obra,* 35: "gozar de las mercaderías."

51. Eltit, *Mano de obra,* 36: "demasiado proclive a la paz y adicto a la corrección,"

52. Virno, "Virtuosity and Revolution," 191.

53. Eltit, *Mano de obra,* 108: "estamos obligados a querernos."

54. Eltit, *Mano de obra,* 26: "examina la precisión de las balanzas, revisa la solvencia y la seguridad de los estantes, aprieta las frutas, huele la carne, calcula la vigencia y el espesor de la leche. Sí, sí, sí, eso es lo que está haciendo. Viene al súper a oler, respirar, auscultar, sobar, golpear, agacharse, esconderse, interceptar, intentar entrar en las bodegas o espiar mi nombre en el delantal."

55. Fredric Jameson's "Culture and Finance Capital" develops this interpretation of literary realism.

56. Eltit, *Mano de obra,* 15: "mística contaminada"; "Tocan los productos

igual que si rozaran a Dios. Los acarician con una devoción fanática (y religiosamente precipitada)."

Chapter 3. Restitution, Memory, and the Market

1. Brett Levinson, *The Ends of Literature: The Latin American "Boom" in the Neoliberal Marketplace* (Stanford: Stanford University Press, 2001), 34.

2. The final report includes the testimonies of over thirty-five thousand victims outlining in excruciating detail the principal forms of torture used during the military regime. It also specifies the twelve hundred locations where torture took place and mentions the institutional affiliation of those who inflicted the torture (military, police, and intelligence officials). The names of the individual torturers were withheld. The report also includes a proposal for moral and material reparations. Besides the creation of a National Institute of Human Rights, the report suggests financial compensation where each victim would receive annual pensions of between 1,350,000 and 1,550,00 Chilean pesos (approximately US$2,300 and US$2,600). Chileans born in prison or detained with their parents would receive a one-time payment of 4,000,000 pesos (approximately US$6,800), and provisions are outlined for guaranteed access to health care and education. These symbolic and financial reparations, which then-president Ricardo Lagos defined as an "austere and symbolic" recompense, proved controversial and led to the publication of alternative reports such as the National Organization of Ex-Political Prisoners' "We, the Victims, Accuse," a 500-page report that includes the testimonies of the victims along with the names of more than two thousand civilian and military personnel claimed to be responsible for their abuse.

3. Representative examples of the Chilean dictatorship and postdictatorship documentary include: Miguel Littin's *Acta general de Chile* (1990); Patricio Guzmán's cycle of documentaries on the coup, which spans from *Batalla de Chile* (1975, 1976, 1978) to *Chile, Obstinate Memory* (1997), *The Pinochet Case* (2001), and *Salvador Allende* (2003); Patricio Henriquez's *11 de Septiember, 1973: el ultimo combate de Salvador Allende* (1998); Gastón Ancelovici's *Chacabuco* (2001); Carmen Luz Parot's *Estadio Nacional;* and Silvio Caiozzi's *Fernando ha vuelto* (1998).

4. Quoted in Rolf Tiedemann, "Historical Materialism or Political Messianism? An Interpretation of the Theses 'On the Concept of History,'" *Philosophical Forum* 15, nos. 1–2 (1983–84): 77.

5. Karl Marx, "The Eighteenth Brumaire of Louis Bonaparte," in *The Marx-Engels Reader,* ed. Robert C. Tucker (New York: Norton, 1978), 595–97.

6. Milan Kundera, *The Book of Laughter and Forgetting,* trans. Michael Henry Heim (New York: Penguin Books, 1986), 3.

7. Jonathan Boyarin, "Space, Time and the Politics of Memory," in *Remapping Memory: The Politics of Timespace,* ed. Jonathan Boyarin (Minneapolis: University of Minnesota Press, 1994), 13.

8. Walter Benjamin, "Theses on the Philosophy of History," in *Illuminations,* 255.

9. Benjamin, "Theses on the Philosophy of History," 255.

10. Andrea Huyssen, "Present Pasts: Media, Politics, Amnesia," in *Globalization,* ed. Arjun Appadurai (Durham: Duke University Press, 2001), 25.

11. Huyssen, "Present Pasts," 6.

12. Lessie Jo Frazier, "'Subverted Memories': Countermourning as Political Action in Chile," in *Acts of Memory,* ed. Mieke Bal, Jonathan Crewe, and Leo Spitzer (Hanover: University Press of New England, 1999), 105–19.

13. Frazier, "'Subverted Memories,'" 108.

14. José Joaquín Brunner, *Un espejo trizado: ensayos sobre culturas y políticas culturales* (Santiago: FLACSO, 1988), 98: "La experiencia simbólica de la democracia se transforma en el eje central de una memoria colectiva."

15. Frazier, "'Subverted Memories,'" 105.

16. This team included the crew who had worked with Guzmán on the earlier films *El primer año* and *La respuesta de Octubre* (Müller, Menz, and Pino), along with Angelina Vázquez.

17. This insight has been developed by Julianne Burton and by Ana M. Lopez. In her book *The New Latin American Cinema* (Champaign: University of Illinois Press, 1991) Lopez has gone on to develop this insight into the more general thesis that one of the central characteristics of the New Latin American cinema is its combination of fictional and documentary representational strategies and that this is the result of an attempt to change the social function of cinema.

18. For a discussion of the importance of these elements in Pontecorvos's film see Ella Shohat and Robert Stam, *Unthinking Eurocentrism: Multiculturalism and the Media* (London: Routledge, 1994), 251–56.

19. After smuggling the footage and magnetic sound recordings out of Chile, Equipo Tercer Año completed the film at the Cuban film institute (Instituto Cubano de Arte e Industria Cinematográficos) with the assistance of, among others, Julio García Espinosa, Pedro Chaskel, and Marta Harnecker. For a description of the production process, I defer to Jorge Ruffinelli's book, which provides a detailed biography of Guzmán and a descriptive account of his films.

20. Marx, "Eighteenth Brumaire of Louis Bonaparte," 595.

21. Willy Thayer, *La crisis no moderna de la universidad moderna* (Santiago: Editorial Cuarto Propio, 1996), 169: "Es probable que el recelo con el vocablo transición' provenga de que lo usamos—no inocentemente—para referir un estado de cosas respecto del cual, sabemos, no transita ni está en vías de ello; estado de cosas del que presentimos no sufrirá traslación alguna, o que ya transitó definitivamente, y que a partir de éste, su último tránsito, nunca más transitará, amenazándonos con su estadía definitiva."

22. The ideological rift alluded to here is one between the disparate discourses dwelling under the rubric *crítica cultural* and what is perceived by some to be the official transition discourse articulated by the state and the social sciences, which beginning in 1990 became indistinguishable as many of the intellectuals associated with organizations such as FLACSO were incorporated into the first transition government. The latter social-scientific discourse has been critiqued for espousing political consensus and reconciliation at the expense of human rights advocacy; for attempting to smooth over the contradictions of a pacted transition to democracy fraught with impunity and simulated justice; and for working to legitimate and administrate an economic model that it had previously criticized. One of the crucial texts for understanding the tensions and conflicts between the social sciences and the Avanzada is the FLACSO document *Arte en Chile desde 1973. Escena de avanzada y sociedad.* This publication emerged out of the seminar organized around Nelly Richard's *Márgenes e Institución. Arte en Chile Desde 1973,* special issue of *Art and Text* 21 (May–July 1986), which brought the two groups together. See specifically Martin Hopenhayn's contribution, "¿Qué tienen contra los sociólogos?"

23. "Puede ser . . . pero tengo mis dudas."

24. Quoted in Tiedemann, "Historical Materialism or Political Messianism?" 77.

25. Thomas Miller Klubock, "History and Memory in Neoliberal Chile: Patricio Guzmán's *Obstinate Memory* and *The Battle of Chile,*" *Radical History Review* 85 (2003): 276.

26. It is useful to situate—without reducing—Klubock's intervention in the field of Chilean memory politics within a larger institutional move among some historians against the perceived boom in memory studies. One of the key figures here is Kerwin Lee Klein (see in particular his essay in the special issue of *Representations* on memory and historical discourse, where in the introduction Thomas Laquer dismisses memory as merely a fashionable commodity, a doppelgänger of identity, and the mantra of an age obsessed with memorialization). Klein gives some background to the emergence of *memory*

as a keyword in contemporary history and cultural criticism. The two basic questions he addresses are: Why is there a reemergence of memory in the 1980s and 1990s? And how is this postmodern notion of memory different from the notions of memory and "collective memory" articulated by earlier thinkers such as Bergson, Freud, Hofmannsthal, Halbwach, Yerushalmi, and Nora? Conflating the rise of memory studies with the rise of theory, Klein's criticism is that the antihumanist critiques of metaphysics that have taken up *memory* as a keyword are contaminated with words like *aura, jetztzeit, messianic, trauma, mourning, sublime, apocalypse, fragment, identity, redemption, healing, catharsis, cure, ritual, piety, soul,* etc. These are words that, according to Klein, don't belong in the vocabulary of a secular critical practice. Suspicious of the quasi-religious and quasi-metaphysical elements around memory (and, by extension, around theory), Klein ends with a rhetorical question: is memory simply a therapeutic alternative to historical discourse? See Kerwin Lee Klein, "On the Emergence of Memory in Historical Discourse," *Representations* 69 (2000): 127–50.

27. Eltit, *El padre mío*, 17: "Es una honda crisis del lenguaje, una infección en la memoria, una desarticulación de todas las ideologías. Es una pena, pensé. Es Chile, pensé."

28. Carlos Pérez Villalobos, "La edición de la memoria; *La batalla de Chile, La memoria obstinada y El caso Pinochet,*" in *Pensar en/la Postdictadura* (Santiago: Editorial Cuarto Propio, 2001), 300: "toda esperanza reside en conserver la memoria de lo perdido y lo desaparecido. La memoria es el único contratiempo posible para resistirse a la confiscación de la vida por el Mercado."

29. Thayer, *La crisis no moderna de la universidad moderna,* 176: "Transición nombra propiamente para 'nosotros', entonces, no la transferencia de la administración gubernamental de la dictadura a la democracia, sino la transformación de la economía y la política que la dictadura operó: el desplazamiento del Estado como centro-sujeto de la historia nacional, al mercado ex-céntrico post-estatal y post-nacional."

30. Michael Ondaatje, *Anil's Ghost* (Toronto: Vintage Canada Editions, 2001), 55.

31. Ondaatje, *Anil's Ghost,* 56.

32. Ondaatje, *Anil's Ghost,* 156.

33. Ondaatje, *Anil's Ghost,* 55.

34. Patrick Dove, "*Exígele lo nuestro:* Deconstruction, Restitution and the Demand of Speech in *Pedro Páramo,*" *Journal of Latin American Cultural Studies* 10, no. 1 (2001): 32.

35. *Fernando ha vuelto,* dir. Silvio Caiozzi, videocassette, 31 min. (Andrea Films, 1998): "Tenemos todas las pruebas, pero no se puede hacer nada."

36. *Fernando ha vuelto:* "sirve para la historia, no para la justicia."

37. Pérez Villalobos, "La edición de la memoria," 311: "en el documental de Caiozzi la exhumación de restos pareciera quedar del lado de la catástrofe natural, ausente de todo contenido político."

38. Francine Masiello, *The Art of Transition: Neoliberalism and Latin American Culture* (Durham: Duke University Press, 2002), 1.

39. Masiello, *Art of Transition,* 3.

40. Masiello, *Art of Transition,* 13.

41. Alberto Moreiras, *The Exhaustion of Difference: The Politics of Latin American Cultural Studies* (Durham: Duke University Press, 2001), 38.

42. Elazar Barkan, *The Guilt of Nations: Restitution and Negotiating Historical Injustices* (Baltimore: Johns Hopkins Press, 2000), xxxix.

43. Ana Lopez, "*The Battle of Chile:* Documentary, Political Process, and Representation," in *The Social Documentary in Latin America,* ed. Julianne Burton (Pittsburgh: University of Pittsburgh Press, 1990), 267–88.

Chapter 4. Critical Visuality or Global Subsumption?

1. Besides Foucault's essays "Governmentality," "La phobie d'etat," "Security, Territory, and Population," and "The Birth of Biopolitics" see *Birth of Biopolitics.*

2. Michel Foucault, "The Birth of Biopolitics," in Michel Foucault, *Ethics: Subjectivity and Truth* (New York: New York Press, 1997), 79.

3. Gary Becker, *The Essence of Becker* (Stanford: Stanford University Press, 1995), 19.

4. Becker, *Essence of Becker,* 378.

5. Foucault, *History of Sexuality, Vol. 1,* 143.

6. Giorgio Agamben, *Homo Sacer: Sovereign Power and Bare Life,* trans. Daniel Heller-Roazen (Stanford: Stanford University Press, 1998), 9.

7. Hernán Valdés, *Tejas verdes* (Santiago: Lom Ediciones, 1996), 19: "eramos sobrevivientes de proyectos muertos, de sentimientos rotos."

8. Ariel Dorfman, *Some Write to the Future: Essays on Contemporary Latin American Fiction* (Durham: Duke University Press, 1991), 171.

9. Valdés, *Tejas verdes,* 68: "En cualquier caso, pareciera que como no pudimos o no nos fue permitido asumir toda nuestra potencial responsabilidad política en estos últimos tres años, así también ahora, como en revancha, nos negáramos a aceptar la responsabilidad del fracaso, a encarnarla."

10. Valdés, *Tejas verdes,* 69: "En el mejor caso, individuos aislados, ocupándonos oscuramente de mantener nuestras vidas. Melancólicos de lo que no supimos hacer con la historia."

11. Valdés, *Tejas verdes,* 154: "Echo a andar, sin mirar por dónde ha ido el es-

pañol, sin volverme para observar el camión, que ha partido en seguida, ando cada vez más rápidamente, sin mirar hacia atrás, sin ver a nadie, mareado por este espacio que hay hacia adelante—es una calle desconocida-, a toda prisa, reteniéndome para no correr y a la vez para no volver la cabeza hacia atrás."

12. The most influential of these include Osvaldo Aguiló, Fernando Balcells, Ronald Kay, Patricio Marchant, Justo Mellado, Gonzalo Muñoz, Pablo Oyarzún, Nelly Richard, Willy Thayer, and Adriana Valdés.

13. The conflict here can be understood as a clash between the refractory politics of the Avanzada and the exiles' attempt to reclaim the historical project and the national spaces from which they had so violently been separated. See, e.g., Gonzalo Millan's critique of the poets associated with the Avanzanda (Zurita, Muñoz, and Maquieira) for their supposed tabula rasa ideals. Although not articulated by a returning exile, one of the strongest expressions of this position can be found in Hernán Vidal's sweeping condemnation of Chilean neo-avant-gardism (represented for him by the writers who have published in the *Revista de Crítica Cultura*) as a postmodern escape from the political.

An important exception to this familiar periodization of the Avanzada (the first move is usually to contrast it with the Popular Unity art scene, then establish its emergence as being marked by the institutional catastrophe effected by the military coup, and finally claim it to be superseded by the postmodern return to the pictorial) is Pablo Oyarzún's important essay "Arte en Chile de veinte, treinta años," *Georgia Series on Hispanic Thought* 22–25 (1987): 291–324, which argues the need for a longer periodization (back to the late 1950s and focusing specifically on the *art informel*-inspired Grupo Signo) in order to account for the distinct processes of modernization that Chilean visual arts has experienced.

14. CADA (Colectivo de acciones de arte) was an interdisciplinary group that included among its members the artists Lotty Rosenfeld and Juan Castillo, the sociologist Fernando Balcells, the poet Raúl Zurita, and the novelist Diamela Eltit. The content of the flyers, reproduced in the magazine *Apsi* (July 1981), read: "el trabajo de ampliación de los niveles habituales de vida es el único montaje de arte válido/la única exposición/la única obra de arte que vale; cada hombre que trabaja para la ampliación aunque sea mental de sus espacios de vida es un artista."

15. Richard, *Márgenes e Institución,* 3: "la acuñación del término Escena de Avanzada buscaba: 1) destacar lo precursor de un trabajo—batallante—con el arte y sobre el arte que, efectivamente, participaba del ánimo vanguardista de *experimentación formal y politización de lo estético*; 2) tomar distancia con la epopeya modernista de la Vanguardia que internacionalizan las histo-

rias del arte metropolitano, destacando la *especificidad local de una escena de emergencia.*"

16. For a detailed account of the Avanzada's ample sphere of influence, which included the essay, poetry, the novel, film, and performance actions, see Osvaldo Aguiló's book *Propuestas neovanguardistas en la plástica chilena* (Santiago: CENECA, 1983).

17. Ana Dopico, "*Imbunches* and Other Monsters: Enemy Legends and Underground Histories in José Donoso and Catalina Parra," *Journal of Latin American Cultural Studies* 10, no. 3 (2001): 333.

18. Dopico, "*Imbunches* and Other Monsters," 333.

19. This twenty-four-work exhibition and its catalog (which was designed by the artist and included original collages and different versions of the *imbunche* legend) are generally considered to be one of the most important public displays of politicized art during the Pinochet dictatorship. Moving away from a straightforward contestatory art, Parra develops coded representations that are not detected by the authorities. Evidence of this is the positive review of the event published in the newspaper *El Mercurio* by the art critic Waldemar Sommer, who praises Parra's visceral aggressiveness without making any connections between her work and the Chilean political context. For commentary on this exhibit, including the observation about Sommer, see Ronald Christ, "Fantasmas pretéritos / (preterite ghosts)," in *Catalina Parra: Imbunches* (Santiago: Galería Época, Orrego Luco 50, Oct.–Nov. 1977), 18–19; Ronald Christ, "Unornamental Variations," in *Catalina Parra: The Human Touch* (New York: Intar Gallery, 1991); Eugenio Dittborn, "Imbunches Catalina Parra: Análisis," in *Catalina Parra: Imbunches,* 4; Nelly Richard, "Hilvanar el sentido, rasgar la noticia, fisurar el poder, alertar la mirada," in *Catalina Parra: it's indisputable = es indescutible,* ed. Catalina Parra and Rocio Aranda-Alvarado (New Jersey: Jersey City Museum, 2001); and Julia Herzberg, "Run Away, Run Away / Huye, Huye," in Parra and Aranda-Alvarado, *Catalina Parra: it's indisputable = es indescutible.*

20. Quoted in Catalina Parra and Eugenio Dittborn, *Catalina Parra: Imbunches* (Santiago: Galería Época, 1977), 3: "El *imbunche.* Todo cosido, los ojos, la boca, el culo, el sexo, las narices, los oídos, las manos, las pernas."

21. Although a case could be made for *Coronación* and a few of his later novels such as *La desesperanza* and *Taratuta: Naturaleza muerta con cachimba,* I consider the novels he wrote between 1966 and 1978 to be the strongest expression of his literary project. These include: *El lugar sin límite,* with its representation of the breakdown of social institutions and the destruction of the principle of identity; the dystopic chronicle of an eminent household, *El ob-*

sceno pájaro de la noche, which introduces unparalleled visions of monstrosity (the tortured and sealed bodies of the *imbunches*); and finally *Casa de campo*. with its allegorical and counterallegorical tensions that end in an entombment that prefigures Chile's authoritarian future.

22. Dopico, "*Imbunches* and Other Monsters," 325.

23. Dopico, "*Imbunches* and Other Monsters," 348.

24. According to Ronald Christ, Parra found the unidentified photograph near a Chase Manhattan bank in New York. See "Unornamental Variations," in *Catalina Parra: The Human Touch*, 36.

25. Revealingly, the 1979 introduction of Susan B. Anthony coins proved to be a failure—the coins are now almost out of circulation—because of the dominance of the dematerialized paper dollar. For a more detailed account of the epochal shift from "metallic" to "fiduciary" forms of money, see chapter 1.

26. Richard, "Hilvanar el sentido," 40: "La obra no se refugia en la interioridad de un 'yo' para oponerse al mundo de la visualidad capitalista desde un lenguaje supuestamente no contaminado por sus procedimientos masificadores, sino que construye sus significados de oposición desde la misma materialidad que usan las retóricas visuales del mercado informativo y publicitario para formular sus mensajes de dominancia."

27. Chapter 2 discusses two specific examples of this: human capital and virtuosity.

28. Gayatri Chakravorty Spivak, "Scattered Speculations on the Question of Value," *Diacritics* 15, no. 4 (1985): 78.

29. Spivak, "Scattered Speculations," 84.

30. The "radical critiques" that Spivak is engaging with include what she calls continuist readings of Marx (e.g., Jean-Joseph Goux), along with critiques based on idealist analogies between capital and the subject (e.g., Antonio Negri). In *A Critique of Postcolonial Reason: Toward a History of the Vanishing Present* (Cambridge: Harvard University Press, 2000), Spivak exercises a similar operation on Fredric Jameson's concept of postmodernism. She concludes that one can extend "Jameson's isomorphic practice to say that postmodernism (and postmodernization as postfordism) is related to micro-electronic transnational capitalism rather than multinational late capitalism. And then the International Ladies Garment Workers' Union can reveal to us that hi-tech postfordism is supported, in the lower ranks, by labor practices that would fit right into old-style industrial capitalism" (317).

31. Spivak, "Scattered Speculations," 84.

32. Spivak, "Scattered Speculations," 85.

Chapter 5. Reflections on a Residual Formation

1. The texts that make up this debate include, on Marchant's side: "Jorge Guzman: ¿Diferencias latinoamericanas?" *Estudios Públicos* 18 (1985), 301–8, and "Jorge Guzman: 'filósofo,' 'sicoanalista,' 'detective,'" *Estudios Públicos* 23 (1986), 291–316. On Guzman's side they include: "Patricio Marchant: *Sobre arboles y madres,*" *Estudios Públicos* 22 (1986), 303–13.

2. Jorge Guzman, *Diferencias Latinoamericanas* (Santiago: ECEH, 1984), 7: "En suma, le trastorna la relación con su propio mundo, lo que equivale a hacerle extraño su mundo, hacerlo extraño a él mismo para sí y hacerle sospechosas las herramientas ideológicas, estéticas, epistemológicas que le fabricaron la ilusión en que vivía. Por todo lo cual empieza a parecerle que nada es más digno de estudio que la propia realidad donde siempre ha vivido."

3. Patricio Marchant, "Desolación. Cuestión del nombre de Salvador Allende (1989/90)," in *Escritura y Temblor* (Santiago: Editorial Cuarto Propio, 2000), 214: "Y de la poesía chilena, descubrimiento, en estos años, de la poesía mistraliana: como si ésta hubiera necesitado de la catástrofe nacional para comenzar a ser entendida, en tanto ella-en primer, indiscutido lugar-nos entregara, y así es, los elementos para comenzar esta tarea ineludible: el comentario—en todos los ámbitos de la estancia nacional—de nuestro catástrofe."

4. Marchant, *Sobre arboles y madres,* 110: "escribir sobre el poeta como escribir con ello otra cosa, única manera de leerlo."

5. Marx's discussion of real and formal subsumption can be found in the appendix to volume 1 of *Capital,* "Results of the Immediate Process of Production," which is a discarded draft of the sixth section of volume 1.

6. Marx, *Capital,* 1035.

7. In the Grundrisse this also appears as the "objective socialization of labor," the collective worker, and the global worker.

8. See *South Atlantic Quarterly* 108, no. 2 (2009), dedicated to the topic of immaterial labor.

9. See Pierre Bourdieu and Loïc Wacquant, "Neoliberal Newspeak: Notes on the New Planetary Vulgate," *Radical Philosophy* 108 (2001): 2–7.

BIBLIOGRAPHY

Achugar, Hugo. *Ideologías y estructuras narrativas en José Donoso*. Caracas: Centro de Estudios Rómulo Gallego, 1979.

Adorno, Theodor, et al. *Aesthetics and Politics*. London: Verso, 1977.

Agamben, Giorgio. *Homo Sacer: Sovereign Power and Bare Life*. Trans. Daniel Heller-Roazen. Stanford: Stanford University Press, 1998.

——. *Means without Ends*. Minneapolis: University of Minnesota Press, 2000.

Aguiló, Osvaldo. *Propuestas neovanguardistas en la plástica chilena: antecedentes y contexto*. Santiago: CENECA, 1983.

Alonso, Carlos. *Modernity and Autochthony: The Spanish American Regional Novel*. Cambridge: Cambridge University Press, 1990.

Althusser, Louis, and Étienne Balibar. *Reading Capital*. Trans. Ben Brewster. London: Verso, 1999.

Anderson, Perry. "Marshall Berman: Modernity and Revolution." In *A Zone of Engagement*, 25–55. London: Verso, 1992.

Arendt, Hannah. *The Origins of Totalitarianism*. New York: Harcourt, 1973.

Arguedas, José María. *El zorro de arriba y el zorro de abajo*. Paris: ALLCA XX, 1996.

Arrighi, Giovanni. *The Long Twentieth Century: Money, Power, and the Origins of Our Times*. London: Verso, 1999.

Avelar, Idelber. "Dictatorship and Immanence." *Journal of Latin American Cultural Studies* 7, no. 1 (1998): 75–92.

——. *The Untimely Present*. Durham: Duke University Press, 1999.

Barkan, Elazar. *The Guilt of Nations: Restitution and Negotiating Historical Injustices.* Baltimore: Johns Hopkins Press, 2000.

Barthes, Roland. *Camara Lucida.* New York: Hill and Wang, 1981.

Battle of Algiers. Dir. Gillo Pontecorvo. Italy and Algeria: Igor Films, 1967.

Battle of Chile. Dir. Patricio Guzmán. New York: First Run/Icarus Films, 1975, 1976, 1978.

Baudrillard, Jean. "The Trompe-L'oeil." In *Calligram: Essays in New Art History from France,* ed. Norman Bryson, 53–62. New York: Cambridge University Press, 1988.

Becker, Gary. *The Economic Approach to Human Behavior.* Chicago: University of Chicago Press, 1976.

——. *The Essence of Becker.* Stanford: Stanford University Press, 1995.

Benhabib, Seyla. *The Claims of Culture: Equality and Diversity in the Global Era.* Princeton: Princeton University Press, 2002.

Benjamin, Walter. *The Arcades Project.* Trans. Howard Eiland and Kevin McLaughlin. Cambridge: Harvard University Press, 2002.

——. "Central Park." In *Walter Benjamin: Selected Writings,* ed. Howard Eiland and Michael W. Jennings, trans. Edmund Jephcott et al., 161–99. Cambridge: Belknap Press of Harvard University Press, 2002.

——. "Eduard Fuchs, Collector and Historian." In *One Way Street and Other Writings,* trans. Edmund Jephcott and Kingsley Shorter, 349–86. London: Verso, 1985.

——. *Illuminations.* Ed. Hannah Arendt. Trans. Harry Zohn. New York: Schocken Books, 1969.

——. *The Origin of German Tragic Drama.* London: Verso, 1998.

Benn Michaels, Walter. *The Gold Standard and the Logic of Naturalism: American Literature at the Turn of the Century.* Berkeley and Los Angeles: University of California Press, 1987.

Bourdieu, Pierre, and Loïc Wacquant. "Neoliberal Newspeak: Notes on the New Planetary Vulgate." *Radical Philosophy* 108 (2001): 2–7.

Boyarin, Jonathan. "Space, Time and the Politics of Memory." In *Remapping Memory: The Politics of Timespace,* ed. Jonathan Boyarin, 1–38. Minneapolis: University of Minnesota Press, 1994.

Brunner, José Joaquín. *Un espejo trizado: ensayos sobre culturas y políticas culturales.* Santiago: FLACSO, 1988.

Bulmer-Thomas, V., and Maria Antonia Neira Bigorra. *El nuevo modelo económico en América Latina: su efecto en la distribución del ingreso y en la pobreza.* México: Fondo de Cultura Económica, 1997.

Burton, Julianne. *Cinema and Social Change in Latin America.* Austin: University of Texas Press, 1986.

———. "Politics and the Documentary in the People's Chile." *Socialist Review* 35 (1977): 49.

———, ed. *The Social Documentary in Latin America.* Pittsburgh: University of Pittsburgh Press, 1990.

Canclini, Néstor García. *Consumers and Citizens: Globalization and Multicultural Conflicts.* Trans. George Yúdice. Minneapolis: University of Minnesota Press, 2001.

Cánovas, Rodrigo. *Novela chilena: Nuevas generaciones.* Santiago: Ediciones Universidad de Chile, 1997.

Cárcamo-Huechante, Luis. *Tramas del mercado: imaginación economica, cultura pública y literatura en el Chile de fines del siglo veinte.* Santiago: Editorial Cuarto Propio, 2007.

Carpentier, Alejo. *La novela latinoamericana en vísperas de un nuevo siglo.* México: Siglo Veintiuno Editores, 1981.

Catalina Parra: Imbunches. Santiago: Galería Época, Orrego Luco 50, October–November 1977.

Cerda, Carlos. *José Donoso: Originales y metáforas.* Santiago: Planeta, 1988.

Chanan, Michael. *Chilean Cinema.* London: BFI, 1976.

———. *Twenty-Five Years of the New Latin American Cinema.* London: BFI, 1983.

Chile, Obstinate Memory. Dir. Patricio Guzmán. New York: First Run/Icarus Films, 1997.

Christ, Ronald. "Fantasmas pretéritos/(preterite ghosts)." In *Catalina Parra: Imbunches,* 18–19.

———. "Unornamental Variations." In *Catalina Parra: The Human Touch,* 35–41. New York: Intar Gallery, 1991.

Collier, S., and W. Sater. *Chile's Free-Market Miracle: A Second Look.* Oakland: Food First, 1995.

Cornejo Polar, Antonio. "El indigenismo y las Literaturas heterogéneas: su doble estatuto sociocultural." In *Sobre Literatura y Crítica Latinoamericanas,* 67–85. Caracas: Ediciones de la facultad de humanidades y educación Universidad Central de Venezuela, 1982.

———. "José Donoso y los problemas de la nueva narrativa hispanoamericana." In *José Donoso: la destrucción de un mundo,* ed. Antonio Cornejo Polar, 109–22. Buenos Aires: Editorial Fernando García Cambeiro, 1975.

———. "Respuesta a Roberto Paoli." *Revista de crítica literaria latinoamericana* 6, no. 12 (1980): 264–67.

De Castro, Sergio, ed. *El Ladrillo. Bases de la política económica del Gobierno Militar chileno.* Santiago: Centro de Estudios Públicos, 1992.

Deleuze, Gilles. "Postscript on the Societies of Control." *October* 59 (1992): 3–7.

De Man, Paul. "The Rhetoric of Temporality." In *Blindness and Insight: Essays in the Rhetoric of Contemporary Criticism,* 2nd ed., 187–228. Theory and History of Literature, vol. 7. Minneapolis: Minnesota University Press, 1983.

Díaz Eterovic, Ramón. *A la sombra del dinero.* Santiago: LOM Ediciones, 2005.

Dittborn, Eugenio. "Imbunches Catalina Parra: Análisis." In *Catalina Parra: Imbunches,* 4.

Donoso, José. *Casa de campo.* 4th ed. Barcelona: Editorial Seix Barral, 1981.

——. *El jardín de al lado.* Barcelona: Editorial Seix Barral, 1981.

——. *El lugar sin límites.* Mexico: Joaquín Mortiz, 1966.

——. *El obsceno pájaro de la noche.* Barcelona: Editorial Seix Barral, 1970.

——. *Historia personal del boom.* Buenos Aires: Sudamericana/Planeta, 1984.

——. "Límites y horizontes de la novela contemporánea." Interview with David Gallagher. *Estudios Públicos* 43 (1993): 21–26.

——. "Quiero escribir una novela prescindible." Interview with Gonzalo Contreras. *Reseña* 3 (1998): 10–14.

Dopico, Ana. "*Imbunches* and Other Monsters: Enemy Legends and Underground Histories in José Donoso and Catalina Parra." *Journal of Latin American Cultural Studies* 10, no. 3 (2001): 325–51.

Dorfman, Ariel. *Some Write to the Future: Essays on Contemporary Latin American Fiction.* Durham: Duke University Press, 1991.

Dove, Patrick. "*Exígele lo nuestro:* Deconstruction, Restitution and the Demand of Speech in *Pedro Páramo.*" *Journal of Latin American Cultural Studies* 10, no. 1 (2001): 25–44.

Eltit, Diamela. *El padre mío.* Santiago: Francisco Zegers Editor, 1989.

——. *Mano de obra.* Santiago: Seix Barral, 2002.

Feher, Michel. "Self-Appreciation; or, the Aspirations of Human Capital." *Public Culture* 21, no. 1 (2009): 21-41.

Ferguson, Niall. *The Ascent of Money.* New York: Penguin Press, 2008.

Fernando ha vuelto. Dir. Silvio Caiozzi. Videocassette. 31 min. Santiago: Andrea Films, 1998.

Fontaine Talavera, Arturo. *Oír su voz.* Santiago: Planeta, 1992.

——. "Reflexiones sobre ética y mercado." *Estudios Públicos* 10 (1983): 2–12.

——. "Trends toward Globalization in Chile." In *Many Globalizations: Cultural Diversity in the Contemporary World,* ed. Peter L. Berger and Samuel Huntington, 250–95. Oxford: Oxford University Press, 2002.

Foucault, Michel. "The Birth of Biopolitics." In Foucault, *Ethics: Subjectivity and Truth,* 73–80. New York: New York Press, 1997.

——. *The Birth of Biopolitics: Lectures at the Collège de France 1978–1979.* Ed. Michel Senellart. New York: Palgrave Macmillan, 2008.

——. *Defender la sociedad.* Mexico: FCE, 2000.

——. *Ethics: Subjectivity and Truth.* New York: New York Press, 1997.

——. "Governmentality." In *The Foucault Effect: Studies in Governmentality,* 97–104. Chicago: University of Chicago Press, 1991.

——. *The History of Sexuality, Vol. 1.* New York: Vintage, 1990.

——. "La phobie d'etat." *Libération,* 30 June–1 July 1984, 21.

——."Security, Territory, and Population." In Foucault, *Ethics: Subjectivity and Truth,* 67–72.

Frazier, Lessie Jo. "'Subverted Memories': Countermourning as Political Action in Chile." In *Acts of Memory,* ed. Mieke Bal, Jonathan Crewe, and Leo Spitzer, 105–19. Hanover: University Press of New England, 1999.

Freud, Sigmund. "Mourning and Melancholia (1917)." In *General Psychological Theory: Papers on Metapsychology,* ed. Philip Rieff, 164–79. New York: Touchstone, 1997.

Friedman, Milton. *The Essence of Friedman.* Palo Alto: Hoover Institution Press, 1987.

——. *Free to Choose: A Personal Statement.* New York: Harcourt, 1980.

Fuentes, Carlos. *La nueva novela hispanoamericana.* Mexico: Cuadernos de Joaquín Mortiz, 1969.

Gadamer, Hans Georg. *Truth and Method.* New York: Continuum, 2004.

Galende, Federico. "Diagnósticos de época (a propósito de Virno y la 'multitud')." *Revista de crítica cultural* 24 (2004): 23.

——. "La izquierda entre el duelo, la melancolía y el trauma." *Revista de crítica cultural* 7 (1998): 42–47.

Garretón, Manuel Antonio. *Hacia una nueva era política: Estudio sobre las democratizaciones.* Mexico: Fondo de Cultura Económica, 1995.

——. *La faz sumergida del iceberg: Estudios sobre la transformación cultural.* Santiago: CESOC Ediciones, 1993.

Goux, Jean-Joseph. *The Coiners of Language.* Trans. Jennifer Curtiss Gage. Oklahoma Project for Discourse and Theory, vol. 16. Norman: University of Oklahoma Press, 1994.

——. *Symbolic Economies: After Marx and Freud.* Trans. Jennifer Curtiss Gage. Ithaca: Cornell University Press, 1990.

——. "Values and Speculation: The Stock Exchange Paradigm." *Cultural Values* 1, no. 1 (1997): 159–77.

Guzman, Jorge. *Contra el secreto profesional.* Santiago: Editorial Universitaria, 1990.

——. *Diferencias Latinoamericanas.* Santiago: ECEH, 1984.

——. "Patricio Marchant: Sobre arboles y madres." *Estudios Públicos* 22 (1986): 303–13.

Guzmán, Patricio. "Guión esquema del filme." *Cine Cubano* 91–92 (1977): 49–51.

Halpern, Richard. *Shakespeare among the Moderns.* Ithaca: Cornell University Press, 1997.

Harvey, David. *A Brief History of Neoliberalism.* Oxford: Oxford University Press, 2007.

——. *The Condition of Postmodernity: An Enquiry into the Origins of Cultural Change.* Cambridge: Blackwell, 1990.

Herzberg, Julia. "Run Away, Run Away / Huye, Huye." In Parra and Aranda-Alvarado, *Catalina Parra: it's indisputable = es indescutible,* 10–18.

Hinshaw, Randall. *Monetary Reform and the Price of Gold: Alternative Approaches.* Baltimore: Johns Hopkins University Press, 1967.

Hirsch, Marianne. *Family Frames: Photography, Narrative and Postmemory.* Cambridge: Harvard University Press, 1997.

Hopenhayn, Martín. "¿Qué tienen contra los sociólogos?" In *Arte en Chile desde 1973. Escena de avanzada y sociedad,* coord. Nelly Richard, 93–100. Santiago: FLACSO, 1986.

Horkheimer, Max. "Thoughts on Religion." In *Critical Theory: Selected Essays,* 123–56. New York: Continuum Publishers, 1972.

Huneeus, Carlos. *The Pinochet Regime.* Boulder: Lynne Rienner Publishers, 2007.

Huyssen, Andrea. "Present Pasts: Media, Politics, Amnesia." In *Globalization,* ed. Arjun Appadurai, 57–78. Durham: Duke University Press, 2001.

Jameson, Fredric. "Culture and Finance Capital." In *The Cultural Turn: Selected Writings on the Postmodern, 1983–1998,* 136–61. London: Verso, 1998.

——. "From Metaphor to Allegory." In *Anything,* ed. Cynthia C. Davidson, 24–36. New York: MIT Press, 2001.

——. "Globalization and Political Strategy." *New Left Review* 4 (July–August 2000): 49–68.

——. *The Political Unconscious: Narrative as a Socially Symbolic Act.* Ithaca: Cornell University Press, 1981.

——. *Postmodernism; or, The Cultural Logic of Late Capitalism.* Durham: Duke University Press, 1999.

——. "Reflections on the Brecht-Lukács debate." In *The Ideology of Theory Essays 1971–1986: Volume II, The Syntax of History,* 133–47. Theory and History of Literature, vol. 49. Minneapolis: University of Minnesota Press, 1988.

——. *A Singular Modernity: Essay on the Ontology of the Present.* London: Verso, 2002.

Klein, Kerwin Lee. "On the Emergence of Memory in Historical Discourse." *Representations* 69 (2000): 127–50.

Klein, Naomi. *The Shock Doctrine.* New York: Metropolitan Books, 2007.

Klubock, Thomas Miller. "History and Memory in Neoliberal Chile: Patricio Guzmán's *Obstinate Memory* and *The Battle of Chile.*" *Radical History Review* 85 (2003): 272–81.

Kraniauskas, John. "Hybridity in a Transnational Frame: Latin-Americanist and Postcolonial Perspectives on Cultural Studies." *Nepantla: Views from South* 1, no. 1 (2000): 111–37.

Kundera, Milan. *The Book of Laughter and Forgetting.* Trans. Michael Henry Heim. New York: Penguin Books, 1986.

Laquer, Thomas W. "Introduction." *Representations* 69 (Winter 2000): 1–8.

Larsen, Neil. *Determinations: Essays on Theory, Narrative and Nation in the Americas.* London: Verso, 2001.

Leiva, Fernando. *Latin American Neostructuralism: The Contradictions of Post-Neoliberal Development.* Minnesota: University of Minnesota Press, 2008.

Levinson, Brett. *The Ends of Literature: The Latin American "Boom" in the Neoliberal Marketplace.* Stanford: Stanford University Press, 2001.

——. *Market and Thought: Meditations on the Political and the Biopolitical.* New York: Fordham University Press, 2004.

Lopez, Ana M. "*The Battle of Chile*: Documentary, Poltical Process, and Representation." In *The Social Documentary in Latin America,* ed. Julianne Burton, 267–88. Pittsburgh: University of Pittsburgh Press, 1990.

——. *The New Latin American Cinema.* Champaign: University of Illinois Press, 1991.

Luhmann, Niklas. *The Differentiation of Society.* New York: Columbia University Press, 1984.

Lukács, Georg. "The Ideology of Modernism." In *Realism in Our Time: Literature and the Class Struggle,* trans. John Mander and Necke Mander, 597–611. New York: Merlin Press, 1962.

——. "On Walter Benjamin." *New Left Review* 110 (1978): 83–88.

Machuca. Dir. Andrés Woods. 121 min. DVD. Santiago: Tornasel Films, 2004.

Magnarelli, Sharon. *Understanding José Donoso.* Columbia: South Carolina University Press, 1993.

Marchant, Patricio. "Desolación. Cuestión del nombre de Salvador Allende (1989/90)." In *Escritura y Temblor,* 213–34. Santiago: Editorial Cuarto Propio, 2000.

——. "Jorge Guzman: ¿Diferencias latinoamericanas?" *Estudios Públicos* 18 (1985): 301–8.

——. "Jorge Guzman: 'filósofo,' 'sicoanalista,' detective." *Estudios Públicos* 23 (1986): 291–316.

———. *Sobre arboles y madres*. Santiago: Ediciones Gato Murr, 1984.
Martínez, Javier, and Arturo Díaz. *Chile: The Great Transformation*. Washington, DC: Brookings Institute, 1996.
Marx, Karl. *Capital: A Critique of Political Economy*. Vol. 1. Trans. Ben Fowkes. London: Penguin Books, 1990.
———. "The Eighteenth Brumaire of Louis Bonaparte." In *The Marx-Engels Reader*, ed. Robert C. Tucker, 594–617. New York: Norton, 1978
Masiello, Francine. *The Art of Transition: Neoliberalism and Latin American Culture*. Durham: Duke University Press, 2002.
Millan, Gonzalo. *Apsi* 143 (May 1984).
Moreiras, Alberto. *The Exhaustion of Difference: The Politics of Latin American Cultural Studies*. Durham: Duke University Press, 2001.
———. "Postdictadura y reforma del pensamiento." *Revista de crítica cultural* 7 (1993): 27–35.
———. "Ten Notes on Primitive Imperial Accumulation: Ginés de Sepúlveda, Las Casas, Fernández de Oviedo." *Interventions* 2, no. 3 (2000): 343–63.
———. *Tercer espacio: literatura y duelo en América Latina*. Santiago: LOM Ediciones/Universidad Arcis, 1999.
Moreiras, Alberto, and Nelly Richard. *Pensar en/la Postdictadura*. Santiago: Editorial Cuarto Propio, 2001.
Moulian, Tomás. *Chile actual: Anatomía de un mito*. Santiago: LOM, 1997.
Ondaatje, Michael. *Anil's Ghost*. Toronto: Vintage Canada Editions, 2001.
Oyarzún, Pablo. "Arte en Chile de veinte, treinta años." *Georgia Series on Hispanic Thought* 22–25 (1987): 291–324.
———. "Parpadeo y piedad." *Cirugía Plástica* (1989): 32.
Paoli, Roberto. "Sobre el concepto de heterogeneidad: a proposito del indigenismo literario." *Revista de crítica literaria latinoamericana* 6, no. 12 (1980): 257–63.
Parra, Catalina. *Catalina Parra*. New York: Intar Gallery, 1991.
———. *In Praise of Shadows*. New York: Yvonne Seguy Gallery, 1983.
Parra, Catalina, and Roció Aranda-Alvarado. *Catalina Parra: it's indisputable = es indescutible*. New Jersey: Jersey City Museum, 2001.
Parra, Catalina, and Eugenio Dittborn. *Catalina Parra: Imbunches*. Santiago: Galería Época, 1977.
Parra, Catalina, and Coco Fusco. *Catalina Parra: May 6–June 28, 1991*. New York: Intar Gallery, 1991.
Parra, Catalina, and Julia P. Herzberg. *Catalina Parra in Retrospect: Lehman College Art Gallery*. New York: The Gallery, 1991.
Pérez Villalobos, Carlos. "La edición de la memoria; *La batalla de Chile, La me-*

moria obstinada y El caso Pinochet." In *Pensar en/la Postdictadura,* 297–315. Santiago: Editorial Cuarto Propio, 2001.

Piglia, Ricardo. "Roberto Arlt and the Fiction of Money." *Journal of Latin American Cultural Studies* 8, no. 1 (1999): 13–16.

Polanyi, Karl. *The Great Transformation.* Boston: Beacon Press, 1954.

Promis Ojeda, José. "La desintegración del orden en la novela de José Donoso." In *José Donoso: la destrucción de un mundo,* ed. Antonio Cornejo Polar, 17–34. Buenos Aires: Editorial Fernando García Cambeiro, 1975.

Rama, Angel. *Novísimos narradores hispanoamericanos en Marcha.* México: Marcha Editores, 1981.

Read, Jason. *The Micro-Politics of Capital: Marx and the Prehistory of the Present.* New York: State University of New York Press, 2003.

Ricardo, David. *Principles of Political Economy and Taxation.* New York: Prometheus Books, 1996.

Richard, Nelly, coord. *Arte en Chile desde 1973. Escena de avanzada y sociedad.* Santiago: FLACSO, 1986.

——. "Hilvanar el sentido, rasgar la noticia, fisurar el poder, alertar la mirada." In Parra and Aranda-Alvarado *Catalina Parra: it's indisputable = es indescutible.* 39–44.

——. *La insubordinación de los signos.* Santiago: Editorial Cuarto Propio, 1994.

——. "Lo político y lo crítico en el arte." *Revista de crítica cultural* 28 (2004): 14–23.

——. "Notas sobre La Memoria Obstinada" *Revista de crítica cultural* 15 (1997): 54–61.

——. "The Reconfiguration of Post-Dictatorship Critical Thinking." *Journal of Latin American Cultural Studies* 3 (2000): 3–17.

——. *Residuos y metáforas: ensayos de crítica cultural sobre el Chile de la transición.* Santiago: Editorial Cuarto Propio, 1998.

Riesco, Manuel. *Desarrollo del capitalismo en Chile bajo Pinochet.* Santiago: Ediciones ICAL, 1989.

Ruffinelli, Jorge. *Patricio Guzmán.* Madrid: Cátedra, 2001.

Sarduy, Severo. "Escritura/Travestismo." In *Escrito sobre un cuerpo,* 72–74. Buenos Aires: Editorial Sudamericana, 1969.

Shaw, Donald. *The Post-Boom in Spanish American Fiction.* Albany: State University of New York Press, 1998.

Shohat, Ella, and Robert Stam. *Unthinking Eurocentrism: Multiculturalism and the Media.* London: Routledge, 1994.

Simmel, Georg. "Metropolis and Mental Life." In *On Individuality and Social Forms,* ed. Donald Levine, 324–39. Chicago: University of Chicago Press, 1971.

——. *The Philosophy of Money.* London: Routledge, 1978.

Skármeta, Antonio. "Perspectiva de los novísmimos." *Hispamérica* 28 (1981): 49–65.

Spivak, Gayatri Chakravorty. *A Critique of Postcolonial Reason: Toward a History of the Vanishing Present.* Cambridge: Harvard University Press, 2000.

——. "Scattered Speculations on the Question of Value." *Diacritics* 15, no. 4 (1985): 73–93.

Swanson, Philip. *José Donoso: The "Boom" and Beyond.* Liverpool: Cairns, 1988.

Thayer, Willy. "El Golpe como consumación de la vanguardia." *Extremoccidente* 1, no. 2 (2003): 54–58.

——. "Fin del 'trabajo intelectual' y fin idealista/capitalista de la historia en la 'era de la subsunción real del capital.' *Espectros y pensamiento utópico. La invención y la herencia: Cuadernos ARCIS-LOM* 2 (n.d): 172–93.

——. *La crisis no moderna de la universidad moderna.* Santiago: Editorial Cuarto Propio, 1996.

——. "Publicaciones sin obra, inscripciones sin acontecimiento: La nueva narrativa, el testimonio." In *Albricia: La novela chilena del fin de siglo,* ed. Verónica Cortínez, 191–209. Santiago: Editorial Cuarto Propio, 2000.

——. "Vanguardia, dictadura, globalización (La serie de las artes visuales en Chile, 1957-2000)." In *Pensar en/la Postdictadura,* 75–89. Santiago: Editorial Cuarto Propio, 2001.

Tiedemann, Rolf. "Historical Materialism or Political Messianism? An Interpretation of the Theses 'On the Concept of History.'" *Philosophical Forum.* 15, nos. 1–2 (1983–84): 71–104.

Tironi, Eugenio. *El regimen autoritario: Para una sociología de Pinochet.* Santiago: Dolmen Ediciones, 1999.

Uribe, Armando. *Primera Linea.* 2002. http://www.primeralinea.cl/p4_plinea/site/20020818/pags/19800102122312.html.

Valdés, Adriana. *Composición de lugar.* Santiago: Editorial Universitaria, 1996.

——. "El jardín de al lado." *Revista Mensaje,* 301 (August 1981): 35–39.

Valdés, Hernán. *Tejas verdes.* Santiago: Lom Ediciones, 1996.

Valdés, Juan Gabriel. *Pinochet's Economists: The Chicago School in Chile.* Cambridge: Cambridge University Press, 1995.

Valdivia, Verónica. "Estatismo y neoliberalismo: un contrapunto militar. Chile 1973–1979." *Historia* 34,(2001): 167–226.

Viñas, David. *De Sarmiento a Cortázar.* Buenos Aires: Ediciones Siglo Veinte, 1971.

Virno, Paolo. "Virtuosity and Revolution: The Political Theory of Exodus." In *Radical Thought in Italy: A Potential Politics,* ed. Paolo Virno and Michael Hardt, 189–210. Minneapolis: University of Minnesota Press, 1996.

Winn, Peter, ed. *Victims of the Chilean Miracle: Workers and Neoliberalim in the Pinochet Era, 1973–2002*. Durham: Duke University Press, 2004.

Yúdice, George. *El recurso de la cultura: Usos de la cultura en la era global*. Barcelona: Gedisa Editorial, 2002.

——. "Testimonio and Postmodernism." In *The Real Thing: Testimonial Discourse and Latin America,* ed. Georg M. Gugelberger, 42-57. Durham: Duke Universtiy Press, 1996.

Žižek, Slavoj. "Melancholy and the Act." *Critical Inquiry* 26 (Summer 2000): 657–81.

INDEX

abstraction: in *Casa de campo,* 23–24, 27–28, 30–31; finance capital and, 43–44, 50; materiality *vs.,* 30–31, 34–35; speculative *vs.* allegorical, 116–17
accumulation, 14; capitalist, 3, 22, 51, 53–54; primitive, 24–26, 32
advertising, Parra using images of, 100–102
Agamben, Giorgio, 87, 92; on authoritarianism's relation to neoliberalism, 8–9; on concentration camps, 91, 93
agrarian reform, 49–50, 120n11
agriculture, 25; land speculation and, 49–50; nostalgia for, 14, 45
A la sombra del dinero (Díaz Eterovic), 12, 114–15
Alessandri, Jorge, 52
allegory: *Casa de campo* as, 2–3, 15, 24–26, 32–33; failure of, 2–3, 14, 37–38; re-establishing materiality *vs.,* 36–37; relation to commodity form, 34–35; time in, 35–36; as transitional mode of thinking, 33–36
Allende, Salvador: in *The Battle of Chile,* 84–85; bodyguards of, 71–74; Guzmán's documentary on, 84–85
All That Is Solid Melts into Air (Berman), 18–19
Altamirano, Carlos, 96
Anderson, Perry, 18–20
Anil's Ghost (Ondaatje), 78–79, 82
The Arcades Project (Benjamin), 34
Arendt, Hannah, 91, 94
Arguedas, José María, 21–22
artists/writers: Donoso's challenge to, 10–11, 117; return of exiled, 96, 135n13
arts: mainstream *vs.* Avanzada, 96–97; periodizations of, 135n13; in politics of memory, 82; state *vs.,* 54
authoritarianism: *El ladrillo* promoting, 53; underlying neoliberalism, 8–9, 48, 53–54, 128n36
avant-garde, 96, 104–5
Avanzada, 95–97, 100, 135n13
Avelar, Idelber, 34
Ay Sudamérica! action, 96

Balcells, Fernando, 135n14
Balzac, Honoré, 46–47
banks, bailout of, 6
bare life, in concentration camps, 92–95
Barkan, Elazar, 83

Baroque era, allegory in, 33–34
The Battle of Algiers (Pontecorvo), 70
The Battle of Chile (Guzmán), 68; *The Battle of Algiers* compared to, 70; collective protagonist in, 84–85; finished in Cuba, 71, 131n19; *Memoria obstinada* compared to, 75–76; used to bridge generations, 71–73
Baudelaire, Charles, 35
Becker, Gary, 8–9, 89–91
Benjamin, Walter, 55, 72; on allegory, 33–36; on completeness of the past, 64–66, 68–69
Berman, Marshall, 18–19
biopolitics: American, 7–8; concentration camp as site of, 91; Foucault on, 48–49, 51–52; neoliberal, 8–9, 87, 91–92
"The Birth of Biopolitics" (Foucault), 88
boom. *See* literary boom
Boyarin, Jonathan, 65–66
Bru, Roser, 96
Brunner, José Joaquín, 67
Buchi, Hernán, 6

Caiozzi, Silvio, 11. *See also Fernando ha vuelto*
Canclini, Néstor García, 41–44
capital, 24; labor subsumed under, 12, 109–15; in Marx's chain of value, 103–4. *See also* human capital
capital flight, 2, 57
capitalism, 50, 112; internalizing of outside, 109–10; primitive accumulation and, 24–26; qualities valued in, 43–44, 47–48, 50–51, 110; transition to, 115–16. *See also* finance capitalism
capitalist accumulation, 3, 22, 51, 53–54
Casa de campo (Donoso), 99, 116, 136n21; abstraction in, 23–24, 27–28, 30–31; as allegory, 15, 31, 35–37; challenge proposed by, 10, 117; *El obsceno pájaro de la noche* transitioning to, 23; identifying allegories in, 32–33; neorealism in, 32; primitive accumulation in, 24–25; realism/modernism tension in, 15–16; showing problem of writing after 1973, 2–3; transition of modernism in, 19–20
Castillo, Juan, 96, 135n14
Castro, Sergio de, 5
Catalina Parra: Imbunches, 97–98, 136n19
Centro de Estudios Públicos, 45
chain of value, Marx's, 103–4
Cheyre, Juan Emilio, 64
"Chicago Boys," 121n13, 127n16
Chicago School: influence on Chile, 5, 52, 87, 121n14; in *Oír su voz,* 47–49; tenets of, 5, 8, 88–89
Chile: Chicago School's influence on, 5, 52, 87, 121n14; debate over restitution in, 63–64; "economic miracle" in, 41, 45; effects of neoliberalism on culture of, 4, 37; as first experiment in neoliberalism, 1–2, 6; Guzmán's return to, 71, 85; ideals *vs.* reality of neoliberalism in, 6–7, 48; neoliberalism seen as model, 10–11; political action in, 66–67; transition to neoliberal capitalism in, 4–5, 11, 69, 115–16
Chile actual: Anatomía de un mito (Moulian), 41
class/status, 47; in *Casa de campo,* 26, 31–32; in Donoso's novels, 15–16; loss of value of, 22, 31–32; in *Machuca,* 39–40
closure, 82, 84, 117
CODELCO, state ownership of, 120n11
The Coiners of Language (Goux), 29–30
Colectivo de Acciones de Arte (CADA), 54, 96, 135n14
collective protagonists, 70, 84–85
collectivism: in Guzmán's work, 75–76; labor under neoliberalism *vs.,* 56–57; lack of, 59, 94
colonialism, in *Casa de campa,* 24–25
commodification, 23, 50, 57; allegory's relation to, 34–35; hoarding and, 27–28; in *Oír su voz,* 45; violence underlying, 40, 62
communication, neoliberal capitalism based on, 2, 9, 14
community, 42, 96; of consumers, 43–44

concentration camps: effects of imprisonment in, 95; as most biopolitical space, 9, 91, 93; National Stadium as, 72
Concertación governments, 6, 120n11
The Conditions of Postmodernity (Harvey), 17
conservatism, Fontaine's, 45–46
consumerism: community of, 43–44; criticism of, 41–42; influence on social relations, 60–61; in *Mano de obra,* 57; in *Oír su voz,* 45
Consumers and Citizens (Canclini), 42–43
consumption, 42–43; cultural images of, 11–12; fetishized, 58; underlying neoliberalism, 2, 9, 14, 41
Cornejo Polar, Antonio, 123n13; on Donoso, 20–22, 97; on Latin American literary heterogeneity, 20–22
Coronación, Este domingo (Donoso), 13, 20
coup, 53; in *The Battle of Chile,* 69–71; *Casa de campo* as allegory of, 2–3, 15, 24–25, 31–33; in documentaries, 39–40, 85; influence on writing, 14, 37, 99, 107; role in democratic project, 54, 86; understandings of, 72, 86, 109. *See also* dictatorship
credit/debt, massification of, 41
criminality, market logic applied to, 90
critical-realist tradition, 14
Cuba, *The Battle of Chile* edited in, 70–71, 131n19
culture, Chile's, 42, 104; economics and, 8, 117; neoliberalism's effects on, 4, 6, 9, 10–11; relation to economics, 2, 7–8; saturation of image in, 11–12
currency. *See* money

deaths and disappearances, 94–95; Truth and Reconciliation Report on, 64; victims of and families, 78–79
debt, 5, 11–12
De Castro, Sergio, 53
dedifferentiation, 7–8, 46, 61–62
defeat, sense of, 93
democracy: collective memory in, 67; transition to, 54, 67, 77
Díaz Eterovic, Ramón, 12, 114–15
dictatorship, 120n11; Avanzada under, 96–97; documentaries on, 64, 85; driving modernity, 11–12, 40; economics and, 52–53, 67, 87–88, 121n13; effects of, 4, 75, 101, 108; fascist biopolitics in, 91–92; memory politics in, 11, 77; in Parra's artwork, 97–98, 101, 136n19; strategies against, 100, 104; as transition, 4, 73. *See also* coup
Diferencias latinoamericanas (Guzman), 106–8
discrimination, market logic applied to, 90–91
Dittborn, Eugenio, 96, 97
documentaries, 64; commodified memory in, 3–4; contrasting styles of, 69–70; *Fernando ha vuelto,* 79–80; in politics of memory, 11, 82–83, 86; preserving memory, 76–77; on restitution, 79–84
Donoso, José, 2; apocalyptic elements in novels of, 20–22; challenge to writers and artists, 10–11, 117; Cornejo Polar on, 20–21, 97; criticisms of, 15–16, 21, 97–98; critique of modernism, 16; influence on *Oír su voz,* 44–45; on limits of allegory, 38; Parra and, 97–100, 104; realism/modernism debate and, 23; realism of, 13–15, 44–45, 104–5; reception of books, 15, 99, 136n21; tension between modernism and realism in novels, 13–18; transition of literary project, 23, 44–45; use of *imbunche,* 4, 11. *See also Casa de campo; El obsceno pájaro de noche*
Dopico, Ana María, 97, 99
Dorfman, Ariel, 93–94
Dove, Patrick, 64, 80

"economic miracle," Chile as, 45
economic text, Marx's, 103–4
economy, 9, 17, 41; in *Casa de campa,* 23–24; Chicago School's influence

on Chile's, 5, 52, 87, 121n14; culture's relation to, 2, 7–8; under dictatorship, 52–53, 67, 87–88, 121n13; *El ladrillo* on, 52–53; in *En la sombra del dinero,* 114–15; entrepreneurship in, 47–49, 54; expanding over social sphere, 2, 49, 51–52, 100, 112; expansion of market into realms beyond, 88–91, 117; state's involvement in, 6, 88; state's relation to, 8, 48; value system of, 47–49, 104. *See also* political economy
"Eduard Fuchs, Collector and Historian" (Benjamin), 64–65
"Eighteenth Brumaire" (Marx), 65, 76–77
El jardin de al lado (Donoso), 99
El ladrillo: Bases de la política económica del Gobierno Militar Chile, 10, 52–53, 128n38
El lugar sin límites (Donoso), 13–14, 136n21
El obsceno pájaro de la noche (Donoso), 4, 16, 136n21; apocalyptic elements in, 20–21; characterizations of, 13–14, 97; Parra using excerpts from, 98–99; transitioning to *Casa de campa,* 23
El padre mío (Eltit), 42–44, 55
Eltit, Diamela, 3, 54, 96, 135n14. *See also El padre mío; Mano de obra*
England, Chilean neoliberalism as model for, 6
En la sombra del dinero (Díaz Eterovic), 114–15
entrepreneurship, 3; emergence of, 47–49, 54
Equipo Tercer Año, 69, 131n19
escena de avanada. See Avanzada
Escoba Cerda, Luis, 6
Europe, crisis of realism in, 17–18

fascism, 55; biopolitics of, 9, 91–92; lack of resistance to, 93–94
father: lacking in Mistral's poetry, 107; parricidal strategy in boom, 14–16, 21
Fernando ha vuelto (Caiozzi), 79–80, 84; criticism of, 81, 117; lack of closure in, 81–82
finance capitalism, 32; abstraction as logic of, 43–44, 50, 116–17; Parra's work commenting on, 101–2; values of, 50–51
financialization, 3
Fontaine Talavera, Arturo, 44–47. *See also Oír su voz*
foreign investors, in *Casa de campo,* 31
forensics, restitution and, 78–84
Foucault, Michel: on biopolitics, 48–49, 51–52, 91–92; on neoliberal biopolitics, 7–8, 87–88; on neoliberalism, 89, 112
Frazier, Lessie Jo, 66–68
freedom, 53; economic liberty *vs.,* 8, 46, 88–89
Freiburg School, 87–88
Frei Montalva government, 120n11
Friedman, Milton, 5–6, 28

Gadamer, Hans-Georg, 33
Gallardo, Carlos, 96
Ganguly, Keya, 112
Garretón, Manuel Antonio, 9
Geiger, Louis-Bertrand, 1
globalization, 103, 111; strategies used against, 100, 104
Goux, Jean-Joseph, 29–30
government. *See* state
Great Depression, 9
Grupo Cine Liberación, 69
Guzman, Jorge, 106–8
Guzmán, Patricio, 11; comparison of documentaries by, 75–76, 84–85; documentaries by, 68–69; style of, 69–70. *See also The Battle of Chile; Memoria obstinada; Salvador Allende*

Halpern, Richard, 35
Hartmann, Geoffrey, 83
Harvey, David, 17
Hinshaw, Randal, 28
Hirsch, Marianne, 71
historicism, *vs.* historical materialism, 72
history, 20, 71; completeness of the past and, 64–65; as nonlinear, 72, 74; recuperation of, 21–22
Homo economicus, 9, 53, 89, 91
Homo sacer, 9, 91, 95

Horkheimer, Max, 64–65, 68, 75
human capital, 3, 9–10, 51, 128n38; labor as, 11, 53; in neoliberal labor logic, 61, 102–3; in *Oír su voz,* 53–54; socialized labor and, 111–12
human rights: documentaries in struggle for, 79–80; legacy of abuse of, 64, 75
The Human Touch (Parra), 101–2
Huyssen, Andreas, 66

identity, 20–22
ideology, leading to coup, 53
image, saturation of, 11–12
imbunches, 101; Donoso's use of, 4, 11; Parra's use of, 4, 11–12, 98–99
import-substitution industrialization: *El ladrillo* on dismantling of, 52–53; neoliberalism as reaction against, 4, 9
industry, 14; deindustrialization and, 2, 41, 61, 102; expansionist imperial period of, 109, 111
intellectuals, 12, 106, 132n22; effects of coup on, 108–9; Sisyphus and, 113–15
International Monetary Fund (IMF), 5

Jameson, Frederic, 7, 34, 137n30; on modernity, 18, 109
juridicial order, suspension of, 92–93, 95
justice, 68, 81, 83

Kay, Ronald, 97
Keynesian state formation, 4–5
Klein, Kerwin Lee, 132n26
Klubock, Thomas Miller, 75–76
Kraniauskas, John, 25
Kundera, Milan, 65

labor: in *Casa de campo,* 25, 32; expansion of workplace into other spheres, 61–62; as human capital, 9–11, 53, 102–3, 111–12; immaterial, 11, 61–62, 111–12; in Marx's chain of value, 103–4; models of, 3, 9, 14, 102; under neoliberalism, 56–57, 102–3; physical *vs.* intellectual, 10, 12, 62, 109, 112–13; in political economy, 51–52; postindustrial, 61, 102; socialized, 111–12, 115; as source of value, 50–51; subsumed under capital, 12, 109–15
labor relations, in *Mano de obra,* 56–58
Lagos, Ricardo, 130n2
La hora de los hornos (Grupo Cine Liberación), 69
language, 32, 43
Larsen, Neil, 47
Latin America, 121n14; heterogeneity of literature of, 20–22, 123n13; Keynesian state formation in, 4–5; literary boom of, 14, 97; realism/modernism debate in, 14, 18; regional nature of literature of, 106–8
Leigh, Gustavo, 121n13
Leppe, Carlos, 96
Levinson, Brett, 63–64
liberalism, 9, 88; classical *vs.* neoliberalism, 8, 89
literary boom, Latin American, 14, 97, 99, 123n4; parricidal strategy of, 15–16, 21
literary criticism: on Donoso's novels, 15–16; of Mistril's poetry, 106; of *Oír su voz,* 46
literature, Latin American: heterogeneity of, 20–22, 123n13; regional nature of, 106–8
Lopez, Ana, 85, 131n17
loss, 43
Löwith, Karl, 94
Luhmann, Niklas, 7
Lukács, Georg, 36–37

Machuca (Wood), 39–40
Malbran, Ernesto, 72
Mano de obra (Eltit), 3, 11, 56, 59–60, 116; dedifferentiation of spheres in, 61–62; labor relations in, 56–58, 61; *Oír su voz* compared to, 61–62
Marchant, Patricio, 1, 108–9
Margins and Institutions (Richard), 95
market, 11; hegemony of, 8, 69, 73, 77, 88–91, 117; logic of, 9, 55; social economy of, 45–46; strategies used against global, 100, 104
Martí Santi, Enrico, 83
Marx, Karl: on chain of value, 103–4;

"Eighteenth Brumaire" by, 65, 76–77; on primitive accumulation, 24–25, 27–28; on socialized labor, 111–12, 115; on subsumption of labor under capital, 12, 109–15
Maseillo, Francine, 82
mass media, 42, 68
materialism, 103; historical, 64–65, 72
materiality, 34–37
melancholy: in *El padre mío,* 55; *Mano de obra* moving out of, 56; in *Memoria obstinada,* 75; mourning *vs.,* 54–55; in *Tejas verdes,* 94
Memoria obstinada (Guzmán), 69, 72–76, 81–82, 84
memory, 83; antidictatorial *vs.* postdictatorial, 84; collective, 67, 75; commodification of, 3, 11; countermemory and, 67–68; documentaries preserving, 76–77; in political action, 68–69; postmemory *vs.,* 71
memory politics, 3–4, 82, 132n26; completeness of the past in, 65–66; counterhegemonic, 68; documentaries in, 11, 71, 77; feasibility of, 74–75; fixation on pasts in, 66–67; limitations of, 86; tasks for, 77–78
Mesa de Dialogo, 64
Mezza, Gonzalo, 96
military, economic visions within, 121n13
Millan, Gonzalo, 135n13
Mistral, Gabriela, 1, 106–9
modernism, 14; Berman's conceptualization of, 18–19; Donoso and, 13, 16, 23; historical crossroads of, 19–20, 22; realism and, 22–23. *See also* realism/modernism debate
modernity, 91, 109; dictatorship driving, 11–12, 40; as Popular Unity project, 40; representations of, 17–18, 98–99, 121n12
modernization, 53, 120n8, 120n11
monetarism, 50–51, 54, 100–101
money, 2, 6, 103; abstraction *vs.* materiality in values, 30–31; in *En la sombra del dinero,* 114–15; labor *vs.,* 50–51; metallic *vs.* fiduciary, 28–29, 101, 137n25
Moreiras, Alberto, 64, 83
Moulian, Tomás, 2, 41–43
mourning, 54–55, 66–68

nationalization, 120n8, 120n11
National Stadium, as concentration camp, 72
Negri, Antonio, 109, 111
neo-avant-gardism, 135n13
neoliberalism, 12, 67, 120n11; authoritarianism underlying, 8–9, 48, 49, 53–54, 128n36; Becker's, 8; biopolitics and, 87, 91–92; Chile as first experiment in, 1–2, 6; Chile's adoption of, 4–6, 10–11, 115–16; classical liberalism *vs.,* 8, 89; dedifferentiation in, 46, 61–62; economization of life under, 51–52, 61–62, 88–89, 100; effects on culture, 4, 10–11, 37, 101; effects on social relations, 58, 75; human capital in, 61, 102–3, 111–12; ideals *vs.* reality of, 6–7; logic of labor in, 56–58, 61, 102–3; tenets of, 5–6, 9, 14; transition to, 2, 9, 11, 24–25; as transition without movement, 73–74; values of, 100–101; violence underlying, 40
neorealism, in *Casa de campo,* 32
Neruda, Pablo, 13
newspapers, in Parra's works, 98, 100–101
nostalgia, 14, 66, 75, 107
novels, 23; crisis of genre, 29–30; experimental *vs.* realist, 13–15

Oír su voz (Fontaine), 3, 6, 11, 101, 116; agriculture boom and land speculation in, 49–50; compared to *Mano de obra,* 61–62; Donoso's influence on, 44–45; on emergence of entrepreneurial class, 47–49; human capital in, 53–54, 61; political economy in, 44–45; realism of, 46–47
Ondaatje, Michael, 78–79
Oyarzún, Pablo, 135n13

Parra, Catalina, 96; avant-garde and, 97, 104–5; exhibitions by, 97–102, 136n19;

The Human Touch series by, 101–2; use of *imbunche* figure, 4, 11–12, 98–99; using Donoso's work, 97–100
past, 83; completeness of, 64–66, 68–69, 75; incompleteness of, 73, 84
Pedro Páramo (Rulfo), 80
Pérez Villalobos, Carlos, 76–77, 81
pictorial, aesthetics of, 96
Pinochet, Augusto, 64, 120n11, 121n13. *See also* dictatorship
Polanyi, Karl, 8
political action: in Guzmán's work, 75–76; memory in, 68–69
political economy, 10–11, 100; labor in, 51–52, 112; in *Oír su voz,* 44–45; primitive accumulation in, 24–26; service sector not understood in, 58–59
politics: of Avanzada, 96–97, 100; biopolitics *vs.,* 92; depoliticization and, 41; market as, 88; total politicization and, 94–95
politics of memory. *See* memory politics
Pontecorvo, Gillo, 70
Popular Unity (Unidad Popular), 96, 119n7, 120n8; *Casa de campo* as allegory of, 15, 24–26, 32–33; in documentaries, 69, 84–85; *Machuca* as revisionist history of, 39; neoliberal project as reaction to, 4–5; reforms of, 40, 52, 70, 120n11; violence ending, 40
postdictatorship scene, 64; melancholy in, 54–55; restitution in, 63, 80–81
post-Fordism: immaterial labor in, 11, 61–62, 102; service sector and, 3, 58
postmemory, 71
Prieto, Ximena, 96
privatization: of public sector, 9, 115; state ownership of CODELCO *vs.,* 120n11

Reagan, Ronald, 6
realism, 37; in *Casa de campo,* 15–16; critiques of, 15, 17; Donoso and, 13–15, 23, 44–45, 97, 104–5; of *El padre mío,* 43; of Fontaine and *Oír su voz,* 46–47; of *Mano de obra,* 60; modernism and, 22–23; resuscitation of, 23, 29, 104–5
realism/modernism debate: crisis of genre of novels and, 29–30; Donoso and, 15–18, 23
reconciliation, 54, 68
refractory, 55, 97
reification, 18
representation, in realism/modernism debate, 17, 29
restitution, 3–4, 11, 117, 130n2; documentaries on, 79–84; forensics and, 78–84; impossibility of, 63–64, 79–81, 86; of the past, 84–85
revolution, allegories of, 35–37
Richard, Nelly, 54–55, 95–97, 102
Rosenfeld, Lotty, 96, 135n14
Ross-Murray Lay-Kim, Guillermo, 67–68
Rulfo, Juan, 80

Salvador Allende (Guzmán), 84
Schultz, Theodore W., 9
service sector, 3; in *Mano de obra,* 56–57, 59
Smith, Adam, 88
Smythe, Francisco, 96
social documentaries, 64
social engineering, in *Oír su voz,* 47–49
social relations, 29, 37, 75, 109; consumerism's influence on, 60–61; market logic applied to, 88–91
social sciences: arts *vs.,* 54; postdictatorship, 55–56, 132n22
Spivak, Gayatri Chakravorty, 103, 137n30
state, 9; culture and, 42, 54; *El ladrillo*'s vision for, 10, 52–53; hegemony of, 69, 73, 77; involvement in economy, 6, 8, 48, 88, 120n11; reduced services from, 41, 89; transition of, 73, 77, 132n22
stock-market model of value, 3
structural reforms, 5
supermarket, 61; *Mano de obra* set in, 57, 59

Tartuta; Naturaleza muerta con cachimba (Donoso), 13
Tejas verdes, Diario de un campo de concentración de Chile (Valdés), 93–94
testimonios, 92; *El padre mío* as, 42–44,

55; *Tejas verdes*'s difference from others, 93
Thatcher, Margaret, 6
Thayer, Willy: on physical *vs.* intellectual labor, 112–13, 115; on transitions, 2, 73–74, 77
Thesis on the Philosophy of History (Benjamin), 65
time, 93; allegorical, 35–36; completeness of the past and, 65–66
torture: defense for, 94; Truth and Reconciliation Report not including, 64; victims of and families, 78–79
totalitarianism, total politicization of life in, 94–95
trade, 5–6, 9, 60
transition, 115, 132n22; allegorical thinking in, 33–34; allegory's failure in, 2–3, 14, 37–38; to democracy, 54, 77; emergence of entrepreneurship, 47–49; mourning in, 67–68; tensions inherent in, 68, 104; without movement, 36, 73–74
transitional texts, *Casa de campo* as, 23–24
Truth and Reconciliation Report, 64

United States, 6–8, 121n14
The Untimely Present (Avelar), 34
Uribe, Armando, 44

Valdés, Hernan, 93–95
Valdés, Juan Gabriel, 52–53, 121n14
Valech Report, 63–64, 130n2
Valente, Ignacio, 33, 46, 125n33
Valenzuela, Ignacio, 73
Vallejo, César, 107
van Hayek, Friedrich, 8
Varga Llosa, Mario, 47
violence, 40, 96; effects of, 79, 82; restitution for state, 78–83; underlying neoliberalism, 40, 62
Virno, Paolo, 58–59
visual arts, Parra's, 11–12, 97–102
Vivanco, Carmen, 74–75, 82

women, as surplus army of labor, 104
Wood, Andrés, 39–40
World Bank, 5

Zurita, Raúl, 96, 135n14